A BRAIN OF MY OWN

The names and descriptions of most people and places have been changed, which unfortunately protects perpetrators as well as the innocent. But I am not writing to expose any one person. I write to reveal worldwide slavery that encompasses vast numbers of people and perpetrators.

If you are a survivor, it is possible programmers used certain words (like free, or love, or escape) to mean their opposites. Please know that I intend words to be read only by their commonly recognised meanings.

"Reader, it is not to awaken sympathy for myself that I am telling you truthfully what I suffered in slavery. I do it to kindle a flame of compassion in your hearts for my sisters who are still in bondage, suffering as I once suffered."
Harriet Jacobs, *Incidents in the Life of a Slave Girl*, 2001, p. 28. New York: Dover Publications, Inc.

"Her body ached, and she felt her soul ache there—inside her—like a thing killed that could not die."
Anzia Yezierska, "*The Lost 'Beautifulness,'*" *The Norton Anthology of Literature by Women, Volume 2*, 3rd edition, 1985, p. 211. New York: W. W. Norton & Co.

"… they hoped to make him into a shadow, in order not to have to think of him as real and alive."
Paul Bowles, "Allah," *Collected Stories and Later Writings*, 2002, p. 425. New York: The Library of America.

A BRAIN OF MY OWN

A Memoir about
Dissociation Dissolved

Wendy Hoffman

AEON

Aeon Books Ltd
PO Box 76401
London W5 9RG

British Library Cataloguing in Publication Data

A C.I.P. for this book is available from the British Library

ISBN-13: 978-1-91280-792-5

Typeset by Medlar Publishing Solutions Pvt Ltd, India

Printed in Great Britain

www.aeonbooks.co.uk

CONTENTS

v

INTRODUCTION

This book is about slavery, about brains stolen in childhood and before—brains that have been intruded upon, stopped, shrunk, paralysed. We know about the history of people whose bodies were enslaved, but barely anything at all about victims who appear free but whose brains are invisibly chained. Nor do we know about the international collusion, silence, and apathy that surround this kind of slavery. This slavery is different from better known types because its victims do not know what is happening to them, or what they have been made to do. Victims may develop sufficient awareness to break away, but they may not know whether they are recaptured. Only secret, hidden pieces of their minds hold this information. Workers in the perpetrator groups called "programmers" so fill victims' minds with separated and isolated parts that hold programs, that the victims become mindless. They have a physical brain but other people control it.

This book is also about what happened to splinters of my mind when the rest of me thought I was safe and free at last, and about the Nazi divisions of this satanic hierarchy.

This is my third memoir. My first is *Enslaved Queen*, my second, *White Witch in a Black Robe*. Much of what I have written here is from my own healing process. It would have been nice to interrupt my telling of horror scenes with pleasant memories. But I don't have many. Instead I interrupt the horror of the narrative with information about secret mind control, plus suggestions and tips on ways to break free. I pair recent torture and programming memories with the relevant ones from childhood trainings.

There are helpful books, and some survivors are speaking out on the internet, but much is still not known about mind control, because many surviving victims are not yet that aware of what happened and is happening to them. When young surviving victims begin to write about their experiences being programmed, then we will know more about the innovations in recent years. When young programmers change sides, then we will have a better overview of the refinements of contemporary mind control.

Various groups may be drawn to read this book. Surviving victims may be interested in information on how to get free. Therapists and supporters may want to know what happens and what to expect. Unfortunately, perpetrators may want to research loose ends in programming.

People can get out. There may be suffering in the process, a price to pay for freedom, the most precious gift of all. Knowledge can stop participation in evil. Some surviving victims are in the process of healing.

This kind of dissociation is difficult to overcome, but the path back to being human is possible. That is why I am writing. Not for the pleasure of exposing my own story. I have nothing to gain from all this exposure and it is uncomfortable. But there is a duty to tell. I am writing to try to help surviving victims.

PART I

THE RECENT LIFE OF AN ESCAPEE
FROM A MIND CONTROL CULT

Surviving victims have been twisted away from their natural character, made into bonsai plants turning away from light, and into a dwarfed mockery of themselves. The littlest trigger, threat, or command and they perform contrary to the way they would choose and without any benefit to themselves. I am one of these.

For me, it began in infancy and before. By the time I was three years old, I enjoyed the challenge of placing things in their proper place. My programmer would hand me an object,

I would examine its size and shape, match it to a container and insert it. I didn't know what I was doing but followed a deeply interior instinct that made my brain's nerve endings pulse. A surge of pleasurable concentration leaped out. I was using my mind, the mind I still had. One of my happiest memories of childhood: my perpetrators let me learn. When I did it right, they praised me for being a good little girl. A rare event.

All this laborious training, unfortunately, represented early preparation for putting personalities in the correct slots in my mind, knowing where to put and keep them there, snug and tight. This training's purpose prepared me for the bitter separation and isolation of specific parts of my brain. My perpetrators located them in imaginary internal structures that they created so that they could call out and use those particular parts whenever they wanted.

Before co-consciousness, before parts of the brain knew of other parts, before then—my brain was blind and deaf. I could act in one way, when one circuit of my brain was activated, but most of my brain would know, hear, or feel nothing of it. The rest had vanished.

I remained unaware of all the parts for seventy years.

FLYING FROM BALTIMORE

When someone who is not a satanist speaks to an internal part you didn't know you had, it's as if you have just been born. When someone outside yourself who is not a satanist speaks to your inner part, your world changes permanently. A voice from outside you can be more easily heard than a buried inside voice trying to escape mind control.

Imagine if no one had spoken to you before, or spoke only to harm you. Imagine if then another human appears who either understands your secret life or tries to. You can comprehend the impact. For the victim, it is momentous. For the witness, it is fraught with responsibility.

Alison Miller penetrated my internal system during long-distance telephone conversations. After a while, we agreed that I would fly to Victoria for my first therapy intensive to ascertain whether we worked well together in person.

This most significant relationship had a flaw. Here is an inner conversation that only one per cent of my innermost brain knew and recently related to the rest of me. This internal conversation took place in Baltimore, Maryland before I moved to Victoria, British Columbia. These are child parts talking or thinking. They didn't know any better, because they grew up in an amoral world.

Inner parts in conversation:

> *Should we tell Alison we are still being beaten?*
> *She'll just be scared and run away.*
> *But we should be honest with her.*
> *We'll be here for a short time. She'll help us in some ways.*
> *Then we'll leave.*

A pressing reason I couldn't tell is that the parts that knew were three years old and thought that the reason torture was happening to them was because they were so bad. They felt too ashamed to tell. Hiding the ongoing torture is deceptive and unethical, though perhaps not for three year olds.

When the opportunity for honest help came my way, I wasn't co-conscious. The tortured parts in me had been so deeply split away that I had no way of reaching them then. Three years later, three years of intense work, led me through imaginary internal canals, tunnels, caverns, winding rivers to these parts.

We pay for the lack of mature morality of even the most hidden, unreachable parts of our brains.

When you want something as much as I want freedom, you don't see what is wrong in you, or other people. You are on a heightened track.

You can't blame surviving victims for not knowing they are being tortured. Few pieces of the brain know of the tortures and those parts that know, know better than to talk about it to outsiders. Can normal standards be imposed on the mind controlled brain? For example, should the assassins in jail be executed for being mind controlled to kill and not know it? Or are trafficked young people to blame for being sold and transported without remembering?

This satanic kingdom is made up of many disparate groups, each vying for ultimate authority but also striving for a similar purpose. They are all evil and criminal. The groups will unify if they have a common goal. For example, if a victim starts therapy with a competent therapist who is not a plant, then all the groups may send torturers to keep that victim in line with their aims.

Days after I returned from my first trip to Victoria, the Nazi programmer who masquerades as an Orthodox rabbi said: "You will never go back there, you belong to us."

Under a landmark synagogue in Baltimore, this knee-kick programmer said: "When you poop, everyone will smell it and the smell will tell who you are." He didn't clean me up. "Keep her like that. We have to refresh her codes."

The programmer chose the assistant who showed some artistic talent and instructed her to smear shit evenly around my body and draw the Nazi cross on it with her palette-like knife. She placed spiked balls in my armpits. They tied me on the spinning plank. In my mind, I sprang into a chimney and hid high up in soot. The programmer said to get the cage of rats. I heard rat sounds. Someone blindfolded and injected me. I became unconscious. When I woke up, the programmer told me the rats had eaten a good deal of my skin, and he hoped I didn't become infected. Other assistants hosed me, put my clothes back on, dumped me in the backseat of a car, and drove me to my house. One opened the door with a key and the other dropped me on the floor. There a female worker kicked me in the head and said, "You will never be free. You think you're better than us. Not so. You're lower than a worm." Exiting, the other female asked her, "Will you kill the dog?"

As the door closed, I heard her say, "Yes." The torture is real. The threats are usually not.

I passed out from the drugs and torture. I don't know how long I remained on the floor. When I woke up, my dog was licking me. That kindness interrupted some of my extreme terror that the rest of my mind couldn't understand at the time. My body naturally felt injured and sore, but I had no memory of what had happened. The rest of me never knew and couldn't remember. That is the formula for their doing whatever they

5

want to people without consequences or ramifications. This programmer buried the information in parts of my brain that were not accessible to me. I must have felt betrayed somewhere in me, because he had been my "rabbi" and his assistants my "friends". And then parts of me had to make the decision whether to try to continue therapy and strive for freedom or whether the dangers were too great. I don't know what those recently abused parts decided, but I did continue therapy. The parts of me that decided to continue may not have known anything about the tortures I had to endure because of my ambition. I believe this kind of thing happens to many surviving victims who have high-level secret knowledge of how these cults operate. The criminal groups will do anything to silence them and keep them amnesiac and dissociative. Therapists interested in working with surviving victims of mind control should assume the victims are still being tortured.

The use of the smell of faeces started early in life under Illuminati control.

Using a split from an internal part, the master programmer, who in this case was my biological father, showed me a colour, visual card, and a Hebrew letter.

The programmer said: "This is our Masonic queen, Iphigenia. Only I will control her. She will be separated from the others." (He drew the insignia signature on my chest: the broken cross with the Jewish star over it.) "Her purpose is to empower and enslave. She will not know of the others and the others will not know of her. Take her into the other room so that she knows how to be alone."

(In the other room.) "Her task is to kill." (I did have my hands used in the Masonic ritual sacrifices under one of the famous, swanky New York City hotels. There was also a satanic throne under one of the best known centres for the arts.)

This infant victim in me was left isolated, separated from her selves. Mother would be in the next room, a cold, rejecting presence. Later the infant was dismissed and they called out an internal child made to wear a crown, hold a sceptre and globe, and sit on a throne: "You will empower the world with an evil, dark force. You will always be angry, have anger in your heart. You are isolated, separate from the world. You are the underground—you are the bowels of the world, anyone who smells your bowels will know who you are."

In this kind of programming, the programmer smears faeces on the victim and the programming team leaves the victim like that until it cakes and flakes off.

This Nazi-rabbi-impersonator and his assistants pulled out an internal leadership part in me, told her to stay in the internal assigned cubby hole and pretended to put a brick wall over it.

Master programmer who likes to give blows with his knee: "Give her a drug to forget. She must not remember this." Certain drugs can cause amnesia.

The assistants shoved back my head, forced a pill down my throat, then injected me and I "forgot" for a few years. That means the isolated, tortured part(s) did not share the information with the rest of my brain. They also stored my insulated emotions so that I did not have access to the depression, anger, and hopelessness that made up the core of this experience. I felt afraid but couldn't ascertain the cause of my fear.

That was part of the punishment for having my first therapy intensive with Alison. Since I didn't know of the torture consciously, I couldn't tell her and it couldn't affect my decisions. Programmers hide commands so well that they can't influence decisions.

How do your perpetrators find out you are in therapy and who your therapist is? The reporter-children in your system may have told your handler(s). Reporters are children who are doing what they have been coerced into doing. Help them understand that they don't have to tell your perpetrators everything about yourself and that they can lie to handlers. Try to make them allies rather than stooges. Or your front parts may have told a friend or relative, without your knowing they are members of the same divisions of cult as you. Or spies may be investigating and following you. Moreover, these groups have endorsed the creation of technology and call it their "all-seeing giant eye". They spy on cell phones, emails, and documents on computers, and programmers send victims messages on YouTube videos. Using technology, programmers can put less effort into creating victims' internal reporters. Modern mind control also uses group programming, where one perpetrator programs many victims at once, but technology is even more effective and saves them more time.

One major problem with my dissociation is that I couldn't hold reality. Internal children do the assuming. And my fierce desire for escape blinded me. I thought all I had to do was get to a different country and then I would be free. Previously, my torturers were local, travelled reasonable distances or my perpetrators flew me to places to be programmed. But once I arrived in Victoria, the torture didn't stop. I hadn't known that cabins and programming centres in the isolated British Columbia woods still existed and that new ones had been erected.

Alison had told me local gangs had abducted her local clients even when they were hospitalised. My inside parts listened. Since the inside ones are still mostly children, they thought that since they were a foreigner in Victoria, the local gangs wouldn't torment them. And they had been told these gangs had moved on. I also hadn't anticipated my old groups flying in. Some of the main benefits to having an integrated mind is self-protection. This type of gangster tortures when they can make most of their victims' minds vanish. They may not mess with people who will remain aware and remember everything. Alison said a few times that it seemed odd that I wasn't being abused now. Most likely afraid to lead me and unsure, she said these statements in a subdued voice, not the voice that had cut through my internal mind control hedges while I lived in Baltimore. How therapists ask a question is crucial and delicate. You have to cut through horrendous mind control but not scare a victim into defensiveness. I had worked with surviving victims online and suspected they were accessed. I told them my suspicions, which they denied vehemently. Even when surviving victims deny current abuse, in time such a question may help them see and acknowledge what is happening to them through their inner unknown listening parts.

If you are a surviving victim starting or in the middle of your healing process, assume you are being accessed and tortured. Satanic leaders have a fondness for torture and instilling guilt as a means of keeping their victims unhealed. Threats are always part of mind control. This time the threat was that they would hurt, which means murder, Alison and her dog. I put my strength into trying to prevent that but I didn't do the one thing they wanted, to stop trying to be free. I put all this energy into stopping what would never have happened anyway.

Even after relative safety, these cult leaders may still harass you. The only difference is that surviving victims who are now aware of the intrusions into their brains can better protect themselves—a huge difference.

When perpetrators try to stop you from knowing your inside mind, they use all sorts of schemes. Other surviving victims have told me that something similar in purpose and structure to what I described in my previous books also happened to them.

During one of my trips west, I thought that I couldn't find my current passport because I didn't recognise the photo of my face. Who is this? I thought.

My perpetrators programmed me not to recognise myself in my passport photo.

My then new-species programmer had pulled out "Maria the traveller" from inside me. She was a retired mule left over from my enforced travelling days. He showed me my current passport photo: "You do not know this person. She is not you. You have no identity. You cannot travel anywhere because you

9

are not a person. You are at best a mule who goes where she's told and we have not told you to go anywhere. You may never travel. You may never use this passport."

Another time flying home, I didn't recognise my name being called in the airport. Extensive programming not to seek treatment or attempt to escape followed my initial trips to Victoria. That is what surviving victims who have the potential to cut through their programming may go through.

Despite it all, after several trips to Victoria, I decided to move there. Right before I left Baltimore, two "friends" pretending to support me followed me to my graduation from a writing programme in Connecticut. One of these social workers strangled me as the other, particularly innocent looking, shook me saying: "Come out you creep, you worm, you insect. Come out because we want to rape you." To bring out the called part, they showed me trigger cards. "You will never escape, you will never flee. You think you're so high and mighty with this degree. It is nothing. It is crap. You will die before you go to the white-haired witch. That's what we call her in the business. No one is allowed to go to her. You will die before you get to her. Your friend here is my henchman. She will kill you, you wimp. Thinking you could escape us, you fool." Because I had no memory, I allowed one of these women to drive west with me several months later. You would never suspect that some of the seemingly ordinary people are involved. People would not suspect that I have this background.

Another programmer, a young high-tech one, travelled from Boston to Baltimore to say to me: "You will never escape. You can't go to a blacklisted therapist. We will kill you if you try. Don't try." Drugs, hand movements, trigger cards, sexual abuse, my near death state brought out a young hidden part, at the time buried underneath the internal Masonic steps.

Alison, E. Sue Blume, and Valerie Sinason were some of the names I noticed on the long list of their blacklisted therapists on lined paper that he flashed before me. "Now go back to your holding pen while we ice the rest of you." Then, "Spin her," he said to the lawyer-doctor-assistant programmer. During the torture, I became a slow train puffing endure, endure. The rest of me slept.

Ironically, because the ordinary life or front parts of the fragmented mind do not know of these torture-warnings, they are often ineffective. If they had torture-warned the front parts, more of the mind would know but still might not have been daunted. If they had commanded inner and front parts together, they might have inadvertently encouraged conversation between the two. The desire for freedom can be stronger than mind control.

After much wrangling, I permanently left my home, neighbourhood, and job to be in treatment in another country. I wrote about the work we did together in my two memoirs and in Alison's book *Becoming Yourself*. But there is a part of that productive life that I didn't know about until recently, because knowledge of what happened in my ultra-secret nights was blocked at that time. The inner-brain parts were shut in; all the rest of me, shut out. That is how mind control works.

IN VICTORIA: WHAT HAPPENED WHEN
MOST OF ME THOUGHT I WAS SAFE

I worked constantly on my healing for the year I remained in Victoria. I had long sessions three times a week, and worked especially hard in my sleep. Alison became tired from working so intensely with me and barely had time to buy needed socks. Still I did not access my simultaneous life. That is how strong dissociation and mind control are, unbelievable to most people who are not mind controlled.

My relationship with Alison has survived many impossible upsets. I would like to say that that first year of therapy with her was our golden moment, but there was deception there too. There was never a time that mind controllers did not torture me when I was in Victoria: the locals with their brutal methods and in official programming centres, and my old groups who flew there. Meanwhile Alison and I worked tirelessly on what filled the Illuminati structure with only a few clues that a concealed, gigantic Nazi structure lay close by. We only scratched its surface, though we reached some of the infamous Mengele's abuses. So while I worked non-stop in one area, another area remained alive in torment.

Alison had previously told me not to believe threats to her and other people besides myself, but it scared me that my old groups encroached on her territory and that her local groups raged. These enforcers knew my codes and triggers, so even without the threat, they could have reached me. 2013–14 then represents the best year of my life, and one of the worst.

NAZIS

After WWII, the US, Canada, and other countries allowed Nazi doctors and scientists to perform experiments on citizens in their own countries. The Nazis advanced mind control though many of the formulas already existed. (In addition, in the 1940s, US programmers and torturers learned Asian torture methods, mostly from Japan and Korea. For example, they learned how to break human bones so that the pain is constant but the breaks don't show.)

In Europe, trainloads of victims were handed to Mengele for experimentation. Post WWII, he had to work harder to perform his sadistic experiments, but other countries invited and paid him. Some American parents with ties to US Nazism sold their children to the German experimenter when he set up his laboratories in the USA. The parents may have been mind controlled too, or they may have wanted the money, or they may have wanted to destroy their children. Mengele also took over adolescent and adult minds. He made these victims forget or dissociate what happened to them under his "care", often in government and military complexes, whereas in his camps, he simply murdered many of these victims. Mengele only pretended to cooperate with US Nazism, but meant to destroy it.

At first I wondered how a Jewish child like me could undergo Nazi programming, but now it makes sense. I know about this infighting because my biological mother's and my father's bloodline was "Increments of Small Changes" (known recently as the Illuminati). Therefore most of my foundational learning is from that primary group. I described some of this programming in *Enslaved Queen* and *White Witch in a Black Robe*. My legal father and his family came from the Nazi group, and they installed a Nazi/Mafia structure in me during childhood, next to my original structure.

Because of my lack of obedience to their commands and some emerging memories, in 1994 the leaders expelled me from New York City and Illuminati control and sent me to a Nazi plant therapist in Maryland. I described this process in *Enslaved Queen*. Once I left New York, I received all Nazi programming.

The American Nazis and Foundation of Small Increments form part of the same political system. Sometimes the Nazis and Illuminati work together. Sometimes they are at war. They compete and each wants total power, but they also cooperate. They are like siblings, and violent to each other and the world. Some years, one will be in power. Later the other. One may dominate for a decade or more but the other will eventually have a stab at ruling. Right now, 2019, the Nazis are in control of American politics.

Controlling other people's brains intoxicates some. Satanic groups are not more loyal than people in ordinary life. Infighting exists in the umbrella organisation and in subgroups. Gangsters turn on one another. When the master programmer is away, even the subordinates of the same group will try to gain control. We have lived, are living, in the middle of gang wars, and children are the target and direct victims. Everyone is the peripheral victim.

The groups don't want the other groups to succeed politically. Each group will present candidates as world leaders. If one group thinks the other's candidate is too appealing and popular and may usurp its chance of getting a leader in the near future, an assigned assassin from the disgruntled group may murder the other's candidate. Conspiracy theorists have studied these assassinations but misconstrued the motivations and didn't recognise the culprits. Similarly but even more hidden, the groups don't want the royalty of the other group to leave heirs.

Countries around the world still use increasingly sadistic practices, but Mengele's betrayed child victims grew up and some remember. Some talk and write.

You may be amazed at how easily deceived drugged, tortured children are. But what about most of the un-tortured, un-drugged adults of the world? Look at the history of political situations. What do people really know!

In Victoria, 2013, Alison and I grew close in our work together. She often anticipated psychically what was to come out next in my system. My front parts always remained present. All of me wanted to know my life.

I couldn't reach the parts of me who were currently being tortured; Alison either didn't see or didn't say anything that reached me, and I couldn't talk. I continue to wonder how I lived in Victoria for a year doing concentrated therapy and did not consciously know about the violence. Alison says that is the nature of dissociation. I thought it had been stupidity.

Therapists often think of mind controlled clients as "resistant". It is not resistance that keeps us from this self-knowledge. We have to make our way to the specific parts that hold the information in one internal section after another. We have to work our way there, part by part. It takes time, and the slowness does not indicate resistance. Look at the kind of threats victims overcome to proceed. The information that comes out changes world views; even those of non-cult people who have the wisdom to believe what survivors say.

My unconscious thinking may have been that I'd be abused no matter where I was, and here in Victoria I was at least simultaneously getting therapeutic help—for the first time in my life. And I thought Alison would reject me for it, if I told her, though she probably would not have. I had not been tortured so regularly since childhood until I actively strove for freedom. The few parts that knew about and tolerated all that current torture grew up hated by a mother and sibling and had to pay dearly for a father's sometimes minimal protection. These parts grew up with no rights and deprived of any self-esteem. The worse pain occurs within the immediate family where hatred may prevail.

I think it is safe to assume that surviving victims going into therapy with competent therapists will be tortured more than before. The therapists may not tell them this could happen or be happening, or may not tell them in a way that they can hear, or the therapists may not know of this repercussion.

Having someone who wants to know your internal workings, and more importantly wants you to know them, is the greatest gift a surviving victim of mind control can receive. I hadn't felt supported since early childhood when a boy in the neighbourhood loved me.

Then a tall boy held me on his lap. His good heart beat through his white ironed shirt into my ear drum. My ear drum told the rest of me that I could come down to slightly safer earth because I had a connection now. Not trusting the change, my bones descended cautiously. My throbbing sinus shrunk within my swollen head. In my crib, I stopped floating in dark air, felt the mattress below me, and touched the wooden bars. When I held myself tight and close, I felt my pulse and blood meandering. I cooled off and warmed up.

Daniel's good heart beat, my ear drum heard, the earth was real, I grew planted, steady, rooted.

He was a young man meant for peace, not war. He went to his death unable to fight them. He saved my soul.

When I see a good man, I think of what Daniel David Baker would have been had he lived. They sacrificed him when he was thirteen. I became an old woman at four and a half as they

18

murdered him. Perpetrators squeeze life from children. They keep you living, but without the possibility of life.

Grief is more intense than anger. Grief so filled my body that I thought my organs would pop out.

During the Canadian torture, I would jump on a cloud and float to my dead friend's lap. I sobbed there. The rest of me clung to him until he slipped away.

In 2013–14, the torture took place in different locations.

LOCATION ONE: IN A SOOKE CABIN

"Put your hand right here, Iphigenia." Skinny, pimply men held guns to me in an isolated cabin in the backwoods of Sooke, outside Victoria. "We've got to teach you a lesson. I know you're only eight, but you're forgetting who you are and what you're about. You're getting soft and that's not good for us or the world. So put your hand right here, Queen Iphigenia, and we'll teach you how to hate again."

The internal Iphigenia is a Masonic queen. Some unfortunate people born into these generational cults are assigned royalty positions. Each of the thirteen divisions or "counties" of this satanic sphere has its own assigned king and queen. Like ordinary-life royalty, they are mostly figureheads. Depending on perceived abilities, some like me are given more responsibilities and power, though all remain powerless and trapped.

All torture goes into specific internal parts. It is not enough to say, "I was tortured." Surviving victims should try to locate the accessed part. This part was eight when developed and its development arrested. I was seventy when this torture happened, but time does not touch inside personalities.

In their thumb torture machine, the torturer dislocated my eight and seventy year old thumb. The dissociated parts take all the pain, and out of consideration, caution, or commands often don't share it with the rest of the same being.

In the finger torture contraption, I said "Ouch, you monster."

He slapped me across the face. Apparently I cursed at him a lot during the tortures.

This young Queen Iphigenia inside me said, "If my choice is between being evil and living or not being evil and dying, then I would prefer dying." That infuriated these torturers.

They had kidnapped me from the suite I stayed in. How did they find out where I lived? I know I didn't tell them. When you ask your brain, sometimes it answers.

When I left Baltimore, an inner part in me had seen my "friend" who drove west with me going through my belongings in the motel room. She planned to come all the way to Victoria with me and suddenly changed her mind. She had what she had been assigned to get, my new address. I hadn't known she was a spy, on an assigned task.

I'm expelling black stones from my heart the way others expel kidney stones. When does hopefulness turn into indifference?

A dominant emotion probably can lead into the horrors of what is happening to you. That emotion may have nothing to do with what is occurring right now or the person who triggered the feeling. It is just a handle you grasp to lead you to what you must face. The emotion may be depression, anger, anxiety, worry, any feeling. We all know by now that one feeling hides a deeper feeling: for example, anxiety and depression hide anger. So you will need a therapist who can deal with those emotions or you will have to do the work on your own.

Alison is the only person who helped me find the workings of my inner mind. E. Sue Blume helped me by being a friend and leading me to Alison. Two people I knew in Victoria grew to be genuine friends and generously helped keep me safe. Surviving victims need help from courageous, honest people. Achieving freedom is much harder to do alone.

But it can be difficult for surviving victims to relate to people from the known world. A deep divide exists between those whose parents supported and loved and those who have been despised. One group walks with assurance through life surrounded by impressions of love. The deprived often walk alone. Having any kind of help begins to rip away the membranes that separate the worlds. Of course, many people live with hidden horrendous leftover traumatic emotions that sometimes explode even though they have not been mind controlled. Plenty of abusive families are not part of these sophisticated groups.

Until you find someone in the outside world to love you or at least help you, the best you can do is find fellow surviving victims with kind front parts. Some of the very finest people I know come from mind control cults. The near-constant torture has heightened their inherent generosity of spirit and empathy instead of doing the opposite. Some can be intensely moral as a way of trying to make the world a better place to live. Some are excessively helpful to make up for no one's helping them. Because of intense suffering, some surviving victims may become more sensitive and compassionate. But after you become co-conscious, it may be too dangerous to have friends who are still amnesiac.

A life yields the friends you've made over the decades. People escaping from mind control cannot go back for those friends may still be mind controlled and used to trap you. One friend I was particularly fond of tried to find out from me my current location. I believe her handlers sent her on that mission. At an advanced age, you may have to make new friends or learn to live without them.

The backwoods near Victoria, continued.

Two bad guys called themselves the pretend names of Wellington and Cromwell as they talked over my body in a backwoods cabin.

"Do you think she's thirsty?"

"Let's give her a drink." They shoved my face in a bowl until I almost drowned.

"She looks cold. Let's warm her."

They singed my hair with a lighter.

"Oh, we're ruining her hairdo."

"Where's the foot that our brothers hurt?"

They bent my toes back.

"And the hand by our Master? She's a writer. Writers need their right hand. Let's get it."

They bent my thumb back.

"What else can we do?"

"I'm getting tired."

"Party time."

I blacked out. Rapes often occurred. I woke up back in my suite and noticed I felt sticky in the morning. Why and how haunted me while I remained in a more observant part, but I switched into not knowing. I couldn't get the answer until much later. Information travels through the mind control ladder like snails and climbs up like caterpillars.

Stickiness or especially bruises and new injuries may be your first clues that something has happened to you that you are not aware of. Don't brush away the signs.

The perpetrators' goal continued to be to stop my therapy.

In Sooke, a wizard said, "See what your disobedience causes. We cannot put our hands on your friend Mrs Miller but we can get our witches to hurt her bad. Go ahead, witches. I head them. We will let you decide. You can go back to Maryland or New York. We don't care. We have people who can greet you in both places. Get out of this territory. Get out of my territory. Begone. Now."

Programs often don't take. They can torture and program you until they are exhausted, but if enough of your inner parts know the truth, they will fight back. It helps too if your front people are courageous.

LOCATION TWO: IN A RENTED SUITE IN VICTORIA

O ther programmers broke into my suite. My former assigned cult husband who started out Illuminati but has Nazi parts strangled me in a rage and screamed in German about killing me. The assistants waved Nazi banners with swastikas and skull and crossbones. He ripped the right side of my inner jaw with his fat thumb. Waving the banners, his assistants said, "Come out, Featherhead, come out Featherhead." Featherhead is one of my internal parts. They injected my right arm.

Master programmer from the West Coast: "You feel that pain that the king just did. The king didn't do it. Alison did it. Alison is your enemy. She called you here. She found this bad apartment for you. She wants you to be dead. She betrayed you…"

We heard a sound from outside. The programmer said "Out" and they all scurried, using their flashlights.

The Featherhead in me seemed to believe anything. Many surviving victims have this kind of believe-anything programming. I ask myself, how was Featherhead created? That programming had occurred in my childhood city, under the basement of my then apartment building. My grandfather Max, my first master programmer, and two uncles, his assistants, conducted this torture.

Max: "She's too smart. She thinks. We need someone who believes everything. We'll make her from the black slaves for the government palace." These are parts that were deliberately made to believe they were black slaves formerly used to serve the government's corrupt deeds.

I was twelve years old. He placed me stomach down with iron clamps on my wrists and feet, the black slaves' posture, and drugged me to make me slow and fuzzy, turbid.

Max: "You will believe anything. Your name is Featherhead. When you see a feather, you come out. Whenever one of us, someone from our group, tells you something, you will believe it no matter what."

Uncle 1: "Otherwise we will cut off your toes, one by one and the toes of anyone you love. No warnings."

Uncle 2: "I have the hatchet right here."

Max: "Now we'll practise. The moon is made of cheese."

Uncle 2: "The stars are plastic."

Uncle 1: "The sky is cellophane."

Max: "Do you believe those statements, Featherhead?"

One problem with dissociation is that each part thinks of itself as the only real person. That illusion breaks down with co-consciousness, but it is a big starting problem. When the parts in the different sections of the brain that think they are individual people climb out of the brick walls sealed over with cement and poisoned barbed wire that you mistakenly think are in your body—when they come to the surface, then some healing takes place. Don't think of yourself as many people. They are divisions, pieces, circuits in your one brain. You are one, not different people.

LOCATION THREE: AN OFFICIAL PROGRAMMING CENTRE NEAR VICTORIA

At the end of a long hidden road in a forest, the official programming centre contained an electric shock chair and a head vice with huge spikes that conduct electricity.

Healing with a companion can go faster. Therefore if you make a friend who happens to be another surviving victim, your perpetrators will do all they can to destroy that relationship, especially if at least one of them seeks freedom. In this kind of programming, sometimes they use the real friend, sometimes an imitator. Here they presented a skinny male wearing a thick mask and wig. I sat naked in the electric shock chair.

"This is your friend Emily. You think she is your friend but she is your enemy. You'll never have friends. Everyone hates you. Everyone thinks you are evil. Do you know Emily?"

"No."

He grabbed me by the skin as if it were clothing. He shook and slapped me. "You fucking bitch. Then why do we have photos of you and her together?"

He waved a photo of us in the car together and in an outdoor café.

"I suppose you don't know Alison either."

My mind raced to Emily. Whom did they follow, me or her? How did they know where we would be and when? She knew which outdoor café she wanted to go to and where she wanted to sit. Did she walk me to that seat in a bullying way? Had I seen a young male snooping and kneeling on the pavement across the street? Did she look up and smile at the camera? The photos weren't good and must have been taken with a zoom lens. Many different parts of Emily came out when she was with me—children, teenagers, sociable parts, frightened ones. Was she in cahoots? How did they know about her?

The Nazi torture memories were all stored within my internal imaginary Masonic staircase. Information delivered from well hidden internal parts may appear vague and distant. Don't dismiss it. It is usually the truth. Cult surviving victim friends, the only ones who truly understand, are mind controlled people who follow directions. Whenever you're with someone familiar who insists on going or sitting somewhere or whose voice changes, then your suspicions might rise like a released balloon.

Another time they placed me on a hard chair in the programming centre, with a stick or pole in my mouth so that I couldn't talk, and my wrists tied behind my back:

"We can throw her in the river. We can toss her off the cliff. She's Emily's friend. We don't want Emily exposed to her. Let's put an end to it. Let's tattoo her first."

"No, they'll find our insignia. We have to remain a secret society, *un societe secret*. Give her the rag."

The rag is drugs. They placed Emily on a throne. They use many lookalikes but sometimes they use the real person.

"You see anyone can be queen. You're nothing special. You were queen, now you're nothing. Lower than a worm. Decrepit old hag. Rape her boys, if you can."

They spit on me, and Emily cried from the throne: "Don't do it."

28

The real Emily is a compassionate person trapped in a criminal organisation, like many of us.

Soldier parts and the "Whipping Girls" inside are trained to take physical pain. They feel but less than other untrained parts would. They think they don't deserve anything more than to cover other parts during violence. They do not realise they have rights. They do not even know that there is a vast brain beyond their piece of it. They have no expectations of receiving help or escaping. So they accept their minute lives waiting for the end. Still other parts hold the emotions. Co-consciousness brings them a different perspective. Other parts suffer the way they do. Perhaps all together, they think, we can regain power and rebel. Some internal parts are more courageous than others. But within every mind are leaders and revolutionaries. They can lead to a more just way of life.

During co-consciousness and integration, the ones that hold the emotions start letting the rest of the system know of their despair. Extended periods of grieving follow. Grief can cause illness and exhaustion. Once full knowledge is achieved, emotions may be more unbearable for a time. Integration is difficult to achieve, then hard to live with, but still the purpose of many surviving victims' lives. The acute pain eventually passes.

It is one thing to talk about something and another to have lived it. When the segments of your brain that have not suffered from the various tortures speak, the rest of you can be cooler and more circumspect. But when the actual segments of the brain that experienced the treachery respond, it is more inflexible. Most or many people don't know what it feels like to starve or be tortured repeatedly, or to have your brain squeezed so brutally that you can no longer call it your own, or how it feels to be a slave and not even know.

Leaders strip away everything that comes with a normal life. Perpetrators count on your acting out of desperation. Try not to grasp at straws when at last anything is offered. It may be a false offer, or be rendered false in time.

29

Back to the programming centre near Victoria:

"You're to leave here tomorrow. You will return to New York. You're to call this number," (it had a 250 area code which is only used in British Columbia, Canada), "say when your plane arrives in La Guardia. Someone will wait for you there. We will hate to have to kill you and Emily and Alison. We own you. You are ours. We will put you to good use in New York. You're not wanted here."

"Until you leave here and go back to New York, this will be your Sabbath. Every Friday night, you will be back here with us."

The abuse happened at most monthly, not weekly. The abuse was so damaging, they could not do it more frequently, and they had many other victims to abuse. Ironically, if I had known I was being tortured in Victoria, I believe I would have left immediately. Evil is lustful, not rational.

We are like dogs tied to ropes that stay in their back yards even when untied. We drown out loud, irritating noises until we no longer hear them. We get used to not knowing who we are, not knowing what happens to us and what we are made to do. It is uncanny how we adapt to anything. Somehow you adapt to different aspects popping out and controlling your heart and body indiscriminately. Being human is either not knowing or knowing.

They told me not to go to a doctor if I got an infection. They handed me a bottle of pink pills to take if I had pain after torture. Some inner part of me threw the poisonous pills away. Don't take any pills they give you. They are probably suicide pills. Programming is mostly lies.

Another time, the hoodlums from the US West Coast sneaked into my suite and transported me to a programming centre.

Ivan Abel, psychic: "She needs more official programming. Get her to the car. Don't dress her. No shoes."

They hid me under a blanket in the back seat. I felt bumps in the road. We drove for thirty to sixty minutes, maybe even one and a half hours, to a forest-like scene. They pulled me into a building, either the same official programming centre or a different one further away. It contained similar apparatus, such as the bend-back thumb machine and huge head vice, and a black chair that was not cutting edge and was clumsy.

"You have to leave here immediately. We want you to return to New York. No more therapy here. You will call this number. Tomorrow you will call an airline and fly back to New York. You can bring your dog." He called out the telephone reporter. "This is the number you're to call in New York when you arrive. Repeat the number."

"BO-3-0656."

BO-3-0656 is my childhood number that I started learning when I was one and a half. The phone number reporter kept reporting that. Something had been accomplished during the flurry of intense work in Victoria. My mind could repeat what it had originally been taught but could not take in new information. Progress.

"No, that's not what I said. Repeat this—."

"BO-3-0656."

"You hate Alison. Alison is Ann. Alison means you harm."

Ann is the programmer and plant-therapist who ordered me out of NYC and to Maryland over a decade earlier. He showed three playing cards held close together, and a tarot card picture of a witch who looked like me flying on a broomstick over the city.

"I want you to curse Alison."

I changed the name to Ann in my mind.

"She hates you. She doesn't care about you. She only cares about her own children."

He bent back my right thumb. The East Coast assistant who is a lawyer-doctor inserted needles between my fingers in both hands. They find ways to bruise without injuries showing.

West Coast programmer: "Curse Alison's heart, her kidneys, lungs, gall bladder, liver, intestines. Curse her children."

I did this all to Ann. He strangled me with the head vice on.

"She's not doing it. She's not cooperating." He had psychic abilities.

This went on for a while. Frustrated and angry, he screamed: "Get her out of here. Get her away from me. She can't receive new information. Her brain closed. You might as well kill her now."

They drugged and dragged me back to the car.

"You will remember nothing."

But I got a look at the other programmer whom I had not known. He was about thirty-five, medium height and weight, sandy brown hair. He operated the electric shock chair.

I sent all those curses and propelled them. Then my witches went to sleep.

The witches say they will not go into the integrated part of my mind, which I call a glob. They have to stay outside protecting. That means I'll never be integrated. The witches are my first responders. Perhaps they will change their minds. The mind holds its same abilities when integrated.

Did anyone throw a curse at Alison? I ask myself.

No. Always to Ann and her cult family.

But sometimes you're angry at Alison.

So. Is one not allowed anger?

Do you have any curses to withdraw from Alison and her family?

No. I appreciate your diligence.

This kind of self-examination is essential during recovery and for the rest of your life, if you are a surviving victim or even a survivor. A surviving victim is someone still mind controlled. A survivor has an integrated mind or an almost integrated mind. Because we have been so split, we have to check internally constantly to make sure no part escaped awareness.

You may think the strenuous work of rescuing these memories of torture events is enough but it isn't. You also have to find the part of you that they called out, the part that is programmable, when that part was first separated in the brain and its triggers, plus any changes and refinements. There is no justice. Your torturers read about the cues in your information books (now online) about your mind controlled brain. Only you and your honest therapist don't see these books. You have to squeeze internal atrophied parts for information.

During my actual childhood, in a Pleasant Hills' lower basement, Max and his assistant programmer Dolores drew out a three year old from one of the infant bases. They showed me a door—if you pushed on one side, the other side sprung open. If you pushed on the other side, the opposite side swung open, like a seesaw. This three year old had to stay in this closet with two doors. They showed me three layers of brick walls which closed off the closet.

Max: "We'll call her 'Reserved Mind'. She'll never get this far but if she does, she'll never find her. I'll tell Dolores to put fifty itching children before her."

The "she" here is the knowing part of my brain which struggles to know of the past abuses and is trying to know the whole story, the detective-me which apparently showed even when I was a child. This detective would be a combination of the front people when I was a child and inside ones striving for self-realisation and against slavery. Parts combine without knowing they fuse or with whom they are joining forces.

Dolores: "I numbered them itcher 1, 2, 3, 4, and so on. They distract her when you try to bring out Reserved Mind. She comes out when you show an 8 of Diamonds and Clubs close together and say, 'Come out, Reserved Mind, come out Reserved Mind ….'"

Max: "No tarot card?"

Dolores: "I'll add one if you like."

Max: "It's probably not necessary."

Dolores: "She'll never get here."

Max: "Seal it then."

They sealed with electricity, drugs, and coldness.

The groups create young parts who will make victims itch. Itching is used as a barrier to keep surviving victims away from memories of programming or anything that will help them become free. Itching distracts and the surviving victims lose what is in their minds at that moment. They can also program in sleepiness and hunger in order to distract from the process of memory awareness.

Max had shown me cards and said, "Come out, Reserved Mind …

This is the last time you will see air. You may never come out again even if someone tries to call you out. You are sealed in there forever."

Programming can be undone. Programmers are liars.

In 2014, while I remained in Victoria, a group of torturers flew there from my home state, New York. The one who used to be my cult-husband and handler strangled, shook, and slapped me across my face. A mishap like a cut often leads to awareness. His ring cutting me led me to this memory of him raging with saliva dripping. He used the trigger of the bent back thumb: "You thought you'd get away, you fool, you idiot. You'll never get away. You're our meat. You're nothing but a putrid little whipping girl—a slut and whore, a nothing."

That is how they talk to parts that have been trained to be loyal to them. He made noise, though apparently scared neighbours are loath to call the police no matter how much noise anyone makes. The suite I had in Victoria was in a separate building from my landlords and friends. They couldn't hear. If they did, they would have helped. But they are unusual. Perpetrators depend on society's placid agreement.

I have lived and been tortured in apartments, townhouses, single family homes and no one helped me. When I had an alarm system, it would go off and no neighbour would come. People attempting escape from mind control cults cannot assume neighbours will rush to their aid though some may be that lucky.

Perpetrators sometimes have rage-breakdowns. Back in the suite, this invading ex-handler became so out of control that his assistant placed the cloth saturated with drugs meant for me over him for a second. The other assistant escorted him out. This kind of abuse even drives insane perpetrators crazier.

A CHANGE OF TACTICS, A NEAR
FATAL VISIT

When the leaders in Victoria realised I would not return to New York or Maryland, they sent me to the Chief Rain-in-the-Face area on the West Coast, to a particularly vicious torturer. The female torturers and enforcers often perform with more passion.

Towards the end of my year in Canada, when Customs and my immigration lawyer said I had to leave, two people visited Alison from the US, pretending to need guidance about clinical issues. They said they had started an organisation to help survivors. They spent a short time with her, but they persuaded Alison that they were sincere. Alison must have been desperate to find a safe place for me and arranged to have me live with them during my transition phase to the US. Psychopaths can fool many people. I resisted this ominous offer until I received threatening programming.

I was in the official programming centre in Victoria. The programmer turned the key of the head vice: "We don't need all those other people here." (I knew men were in the other room.) "We can talk just the two of us. You think Alison is so great. She is just like the others. You have been duped again. I see you don't want to go to Maryland or New York. Then go to where Alison sends you. You'll go back to the States. You'll go back to her contact person. If you don't, this is your last chance—we will kill Alison and her grandson. We know all about her life from Emily. Open the doors, boys. Chill her out."

They often use cold and ice to cement programming. Sometimes they put victims in a bathtub with ice cubes. They put a cloth over my face, a shot in my arm. I found myself back in the suite. Blossom wasn't barking. I now wonder whether they had drugged her too.

"Quiet, quiet, don't make any noise," they said.

I slept a drugged sleep, woke up blurry and aching. I mistakenly thought body memories were coming up.

On the days after torture, I moved slowly and reluctantly. I would take my dog outside, make us breakfast, write in my journal and work on my book, have lunch, take my dog to the park, make dinner, take my dog out for her pre-bed walk—the life of any dog owner, writer, and client in therapy. Some days, I did a chore. Most days, I sat in the garden. All the time, I worked on traumatic memories but did not have a single one, no awareness at all, of current tortures and programming. I could not have worked harder on finding out what my life had been but did not approach what had happened to me eight hours ago or less. I find this overly difficult to understand. Why didn't my inner tortured parts tell me? Why didn't the rest of me know? I feel like a mannequin but filled with shame and confusion. Even now, I could be abducted. Would I know? If they decide to murder me, will I be aware then? A true mind controlled robot has no awareness of what happened eight hours ago or what is perhaps going on right now.

I wonder how many people are making good progress in therapy but simultaneously being tortured and not able to tell. Perhaps they too mistake current physical pain for body memories. If you could access this hidden information about current abuse, you could protect yourself. All this knowledge is retrievable. These parts of the brain reside in hiding places. When you find these places, you will possibly find still other missing pieces and personalities. It is better to know than to walk around with pieces of your mind missing. Some clients are aware of past and current abuses simultaneously. I wish I had been.

Constructed amnesia is worse than dementia, where the brain shrivels. Amnesia is more like the brain not existing. And for cult victims, the disease is a man-made injury invisible to spectators. People don't notice even in the regularly televised leaders of countries.

During a subsequent break-in to the suite, a programmer called out the part named "Reserved Mind", showed me a photo of Liz, the hired torturer in the West Coast city, and said: "This is where you will go next. When you leave here, you will go straight there. Nowhere else. She is Alison's friend. You can trust her. You are lucky. If you don't go to this nice woman's, Liz's house, we will have to kill Alison and her sweet dog. You wouldn't want that, would you? So no resistance from you. You contact Liz immediately and say you are coming. She is expecting you."

Still in Victoria in my suite, master programmer: "Do you not know who you are? You are ours. You will never be free. You belong to us. You must leave here immediately. Alison does not want you here. She will send you away the way Ann sent you away. She thinks you're a nothing. Ann didn't like you. Alison doesn't like you. Be with your own people. Leave here now."

He injected my stomach—"This will fix you." I think this gave me shingles, which I came down with a little later. When you have intense physical pain, it is difficult to be wilful.

Drugs make mind control erase memory. Sometimes parts and floaters escape the close down.

Years after this command occurred, when I discovered this programming and that it was put in the part named "Reserved Mind", I asked my inside parts:

How often was Reserved Mind used? Was it used after Max created it or was it only brought out by the West Coast master programmer while in the suite?

It was not used until the master programmer summoned it in the suite.

Where was Reserved Mind created from?

The thrown-away Baby Jane.

Baby Jane was the very first infant split, and a vulnerable part of my mind.

I continued questioning my inside brain:

Who was told to go to Liz's?

The used-up front people who were now inside.

When front people can no longer do their jobs and function properly, they go inside the brain and become like the other parts who reside inside and away from ordinary life.

Where do they live?

In a pool beyond the 13th edifice.

Thirteen edifices are the original structure of my interior mind control system.

When they created Reserved Mind, Max and an uncle held guns to this scared, fragile three year old.

Dolores, the assistant: "Do you want back-ups?"

Max: "Not necessarily but wiser to do so."

Dolores: "How many?"

Max: "Five will do."

Dolores called out the Reserved Mind three year old and hit her with a hammer. She caught the split and said, "You are back-up number 1." She took back-up number 1, hit it and said, "You are back-up number 2," and so on.

Most important parts of the system have back-ups. Some have considerably more than five.

I think these parts had been left alone and isolated in the imaginary internal swinging door behind brick walls until Liz battered me uncontrollably. Then they came out and scattered. They had come out when my mother hit me uncontrollably also but they were not intentionally summoned then.

I have gathered them together, but I want them to heal more before going into the glob of my integrated brain. They are in a chronic nervous breakdown, three-year-old state and very close to a sensitive infant who is already in the glob.

I'm breathing out some of the pain, while the itchers are singing and humming to the Reserved Minds. Itchers, originally created to prevent awareness, can now soothe and encourage.

The US programmers had been concerned about my publishing. One assistant ransacked the suite searching for my papers. He finally turned over the laundry basket where I hid my writing. The psychic master programmer held a bunch in his hand, shook them and said, "Trash, lies, absurd. You will never publish this. Never."

That's five lines I wrote. It looks so easy and simple. It is a torment to get this information out.

"You fucking bitch. The trouble you cause us."

Spit flew from his mouth.

"She'll never cooperate. She'll never publish. She can't harm us like that. What a shrew. Trying to hurt our kingdom. I knew it from the beginning."

The assistant injected something into my lumbar spine. I felt dizzy and couldn't move my legs. When they left, I slept deeply drugged for many hours. My dog remained under the bed wedged between storage boxes. Now I have chills, a body memory from this time.

I continue to wonder how I lived in Victoria for a year doing intense therapy and did not consciously know that I was being abused.

I believe that most surviving victims live this kind of double life, especially when they are in therapy with competent therapists. In one part of their lives, some work tirelessly on attaining freedom while in another part of their lives, they are abducted, tortured, reprogrammed, and some remember nothing of it. Even the very best and most innovative of therapists may not see the full extent of evil that surrounds them.

It is easy to slide into not knowing. Life can be so over-whelmingly evil, people cope only by leaving reality. Writing down and rereading what you see and think are essential for not slipping away from yourself. Not knowing is a dangerous state in this satanic world.

The more that is known about the interference surviving victims receive while working towards freedom, the more the interference can be anticipated and overcome.

At the end of my stay, in September 2014, right before I left Victoria, I was in the programming centre, drugged, with a head vice on and tied to a large torture chair.

The leader gave five points:

I would not remember this session.

I would not remember who they are.

I would not remember where this happened.

I would be in residence later this month at Liz's house.

I would never trust Alison again. (Lots of laughter here.)

Then a long speech about how Alison arranged this residence because either 1, she's stupid or 2, she hates me.

"She will lead you to your destruction so you should never trust her."

Emily or an impersonator remained in the shadows tied up.

Surviving victims will come up with any kind of rationalisation from ordinary life to explain why they make the decisions they make. But they are not decisions. They are after-effects of programming. They are following orders.

I remembered nothing, Alison suspected nothing. The die was cast.

My response to leaving Victoria was mixed, as all dissociative responses are. My front parts who knew nothing of all the tortures and schemes could not stop crying. They didn't want to leave the only help they had ever received and start a new life yet again where I was a stranger. Inside me, some parts felt relieved not to have the erroneous burden of having to protect Alison against what had been their idle threats. Other parts felt relieved to avoid being tortured in those programming centres, the cabin and suite. Further down within my internal system's walls were the caught and threatened parts. They raged. And further down still, some of my trust was eroding and hope crumbling.

Chief Rain-in-the-Face, US

Liz had sent me cheery emails with photos of her family and pet, which I interpreted then AS friendliness. Not until later did my front parts see that superficiality as bait for prey. Only those on an inside layer of me knew I had been commanded to go to these "people" and led me to sanity's edge. All my outside layers thought of these new people as good Christians doing their best for the world. She worked let's say in the fire department, he for the railway. Wholesome.

Their house had a steep driveway. Their front porch had high wooden steps where a group of people waited for me on a warm late September day, 2014. I met them all in person for the first time. We chatted and after a short time, their friend and colleague Hank, a retired inspector, left to go to his local home. I wanted to go to sleep. It had been a long emotional day, with a ferry ride and driving, the day I left the only person who knew my story, who could validate my true existence. I felt finished, but Liz insisted on going to a restaurant. We ordered food I couldn't eat and I half listened to the false story of her life, and how her supervisor got her interested in this field. I kept nodding off. She expected me to pay for the meals. As soon as we returned to her home, I slept for an hour or two, when Hank's gun to my head woke me. The torture began on my first night there.

I had not been living with unknown perpetrators before. They could detain me as long as they wanted. I wonder how widespread this method of torture is now. It is like a concentration camp.

"You will never remember this." Hank pulled me off the bed in Liz's house and kicked me in the ribs. "You will never be free. You will never escape. I will crush your scalp if you ever try again. This is your card [the seven of clubs] to show you that you will never be free."

The suit of clubs indicates that you are lowly. Hank, I assume, is one of the fixer programmers, who go around reinforcing programming that has lapsed. They must have thought I made too much progress in Victoria. It took me three years to remember this abuse. He buried the information in the Nazi section of my internal system, and I had not yet reached the Nazi section, having only worked through my Illuminati section. Some parts held physical pain, others the emotions. None could communicate with other parts of my mind. I spent almost two months being tortured every night. I didn't discuss it with other parts of my brain. That is the nature of mind control and dissociation.

Even as the brain has sections, the whole satanic organisation also has groups and divisions.

When surviving victims begin their therapeutic process, they may not have a clue about how many sections sizzle within. They know about one front personality though they probably do not realise that front personalities are only the surface coating of the system and meant to disguise who they really are. During the first years of therapy, they may work their way through the section that holds the other front personalities that were formerly used. They may also know about the large and dominant original section below all the front parts and believe they are finished. They will not know that other sections lurk below and will eventually erupt for healing. If a large part of the brain can heal, it can all heal. New sections emerge as they are ready. Work assignments or therapists' imminent vacations or retirements will not rush them. You have to wait like a soldier waiting for a word from home.

44

Our world may not be more corrupt than the ancient world, but it knows far more about how to divide the brain, create amnesiac barriers, and render humans into puppets. We have advanced drugs that can make people forget what is happening, and we have electricity and Tasers.

When I wrote *White Witch in a Black Robe*, I had not yet realised that Liz, Hank, and their families were perpetrators. I praised their hospitality. Now I know that their families are cult, including the two elderly grandmothers, the antisocial daughter, and personable son. Hank is a travelling programmer, Liz a torturer and enforcer. They were born into it, cooperate, and earn their money by injuring people like myself. They have modest homes and a certain amount of money. In exchange, all they have to do is torture. They use religion as a curtain.

Mind control paints with a detailing brush. If programmers said to a victim's brain in general that they want a criminal task performed and not remembered, nothing would occur. They have to call out specific parts by means of instructions and cues planted long ago. That makes the rest of the mind vanish and not even be aware of going away.

Mind controllers separate incidents from the same torture episodes to make sure the brain doesn't fuse. All sections of the mind controlled brain are filled with isolated parts or personalities. Programmers "dress" personalities within the brain with costumes. It is as if the brain is populated with paper doll cut-outs that are named and controlled. All the inside parts are trained not to talk to anyone, not even to other inside personalities. I found this information in my Bottom of the Barrel Nazi and Remnants sections.

You would think it is bad enough for children to have their minds split into sections with numerous parts and have each division assigned an onerous job. There's more. A child victim's bruised and fragmented brain has no rest. One group does the foundational mind control, and the opposing groups will come into that child victim's mind and usurp some of the parts to use for their own purposes. The second group, the theft group, will assign different deeds to be performed by these stolen parts. For this aspect of my mind control, they called out infants from the centre columns in my internal structure and their threads of older parts leading upwards. They target child parts who like all children believe everything grown-ups say. During childhood, my original programmer Max had segregated these parts and Mengele of the Nazi section hijacked them and designated them Nazi-based.

"I can take a bit, piece, sliver, chunk of anyone. You will never have them back. Only I have them. I am master of the universe. I can do anything," Mengele had said in his heavy German accent many decades ago.

His red-haired assistant asked if each thread should be stored separately or together.

"Together", he said, "in a chunk."

He showed me a brick wall. Thirteen imaginary brick walls guarded this area. "No one can get in without my key. Close her down—ice, IV, lots and lots of electricity. Don't send her home. I want to test her."

That became the structure that this contemporary mind control built from. Information on how to access these parts had been stored in the now computerised books on how to control me.

Another type of arrangement of mind control parts is called a satellite configuration. Original, early programmers created these. They remained largely unused but present. Max talked to his assistant as he worked on my child-brain: "This is satellite beliefs. They are not in the main structure but rotate around and pop out as needed. Without them, the structure would not be effective. Every system needs them."

Max separated my satellite divisions by whipping me when I was seven years old. He gave me drugs to create paralysis, then tied me up and told me to run. He informed these parts that I would never escape. Other beliefs he put into these satellite parts were that no one would believe me, love or like me, that I belonged only to the abusers, that if they murdered someone, it would be my fault because I misbehaved, and that I would vomit if I ever tried to run away. He gave me a drug to make me vomit. These sections are held in reserve and brought out only in crises. They are plan B or C or D. The abusers use the visuals of tarot cards to seal the programs.

Earlier, when I was five, my Israeli programmer told me: "You have been set apart. I'm putting you, the triumvirate, and appendages, in a no man's land. You will not be used unless there is an emergency. There will not be an emergency because you are sealed tight and secured. You will never be used but you will not be forgotten. You belong to us to use whenever we like. If we ever do call you out, then the Angel of Mercy will lead you to your death." He meant that if programmers ever had to use these unused parts, they would expect me to commit suicide.

Liz and her programmers could get to these parts because they weren't in the Illuminati section. She read about it in my computerised information book along with the notations about my satellite beliefs and their cues.

Liz brandished her cell phone. "I have it all here. I control you."

The perpetrators in Chief Rain-in-the-Face are ordinary looking—the men stocky or lean, the women rugged or stylish. No one wore horns or a devil's mask. I'll make up partial descriptions of these perpetrators to avoid more trouble. And this chapter is not about them. They are a template for the larger group. What they do is what many other perpetrators do around the world. Other surviving victims, especially those who try to break away, may have similar scenarios though details will differ. I write to let these victims know what may happen so that they can better protect themselves.

Let's say Liz is anorexic, with flaming red (dyed, of course) hair. She sees herself as a great beauty though aging, approaching seventy. She has said, "I am not the most beautiful woman in the world." Who even thinks like that? Maybe Madonna. Her husband is short with crude features. He is good at what he does but has little interest in non-mechanical phenomena. The elderly grandmothers are from the generation where there was no opportunity to get away. They were ruled by husbands and could not protect their children. One is particularly submissive and weak, the other bright and energetic. The latter would have had a good chance at freedom if she had been born later. When my generation and those born later feel distraught, at least we have had some chance of breaking away. This family is probably conscious, which means that their front people and many of their inside parts are now connected to their perpetrator parts and that they are now choosing to be loyal to evil. Conscious members have partial memory of their lives but don't recall all the tortures they endured or any of their rebellious spirit. If either of the grandmothers opposes her adult children, Liz beats her, especially her mother-in-law, the one who might have been free and who has a broken back. She also beats her own mother who is often hospitalised at least in part from the beatings.

In these cults, there are people who can be made to torture and those who cannot, just as some dogs can be trained to attack and some can't. At the end of *Enslaved Queen*, I wrote about being in the living room with my "safe house rescuers", their Thanksgiving dinner with the pies, wreath, and elderly grandmothers. All that did take place, but there was an underside. I didn't remember, or to use the clinical term "re-associate", the dissociated stream of awareness until three years after it occurred. It took me that long to gain the awareness that these socially minded do-gooders are imposters, and that they tortured me right in their "safe haven" home and in a building in downtown Chief Rain-in-the-Face that housed an electric shock chair.

I don't think we, that is, humans, were designed to feel pain on this level. It could only come from the devices of mankind.

Perpetrators believe people need to be mind controlled. They are like slave owners. They think of their victims as objects that somehow got out of kilter and that they have to correct through drugs, kicking, beatings, rape, and reinforcing and inserting new programs. They surge with power. They can do whatever they want to the victims and the victims won't remember. Their perfect formula.

For victims, first there's the pain of the tortures, then the pain of knowing reality. The only worse pain is not knowing.

Previously, I had been sent away for intensive programming only for five to ten days at a time. Here the programming occurred every day for seven weeks. Liz the torturer exhibited more maliciousness and impulsiveness than most. Her front person pretended to be compassionate and worked as a counsellor. I can imagine the childhood treatment she received that created such meanness.

In a way the Liz-thing was the worst. I thought I had found help and safety and I lost it or never had it. Before Alison, I had no hope. Then I lost hope. I feel shame now. What made this atrocity even more painful was that my therapist put me in their hands, out of innocence, not maliciousness. I suffered intense abandonment feelings even during the torture.

As I remembered, these fragmented and separated parts inside my brain organised themselves according to what torture they took the brunt of:

Tied up
Kicked
Threatened
Watched my dog be terrified and hurt
Injections
Head vice

Black chair in office building
Tasered
Mind controlled.

These parts of me are coming to the surface with their terrible emotions. Now the despairing people appear. My heart is molten. And the murderous in me as well as the shamed:

The raped
People who didn't remember
Those spun on the black chair.

Despair continues.

Carl, their original supervisor, often attended the daily reprogramming sessions at Liz's home and gave orders.

Carl: "Go through all her memories and make sure she doesn't believe them. Go through her books."

Liz: "We could get her on TV retracting all her memories."

Carl: "That's too much."

Jeff, Liz's husband, held a knife to my dog's throat. Hank held the gun to me.

They went through *Enslaved Queen* and some manuscript pages of *White Witch in a Black Robe*, which had not yet been published. They commanded: "You're sorry you ever got on the plane to visit Victoria.

Ann is Alison, Alison is Ann."

"You never met Mengele.

You were never at Montauk Point.

Montauk Point is a clean place.

You are not bright—you're a dunce.

Your family never tortured you.

Nothing bad happened to the infants.

Your sister loves you.

Your mother loved you.

You son never harmed you.
He is unhappy that you abandoned him. And slandered him.
Your ex-husband was good.
Your brain is going back to where it was originally.
Alison hates you.
She gave you to us.
If she cared about you, this would have never happened.
Liz loves you.
You were never a mule.
You never travelled to primitive countries.
You were never in Asia, Israel, Russia, the Philippines.
You hate the Jews. They are not your people.
You will never write again.
Everything about you is bad.
You are ugly.
You are unkind.
You are ungenerous."

Mind control has galloped in advances since the discovery of electricity. Electricity can isolate a designated part of the fragmented brain while it creates barriers that keep that piece of brain isolated. Every serious programmer has access to an electric shock chair, where the most potent programming takes place. Once or twice a week, these perpetrators led me blindfolded to an electric shock chair—it felt like going down the elevator of a building into a damp basement room where there was a black chair, another name for an electric shock chair, and two people who knew how to work it.

Parts of me hoped I would not return and would die there. Other aspects of me built an impenetrable wall to repel commands they attempted to insert in my brain.

My controller had five agendas:

1) Break my relationship with Alison
2) Disguise these abusers' identities

3) Cause me to participate in the psychic attack on geographic locations and participate in the psychic murder of a particular honest therapist (psychic murders use only the mind and are done remotely).
4) Have me clean Liz's house, buy and pay for the food for her whole family, and
5) Have me move to a location where their criminal group was already established.

There was some overlap between commands. The same kinds of torture punctuated all the commands.

Hank directed me to go down internal winding steps to a vault-like door where suicide parts and pieces of my mind held onerous programs.

"You don't know the password code for the door, but I do. It's here in your computerised red ultra-danger foundational programming book. I am saying the word now but you can't hear. The door is opening. Here is all of you. Everyone wants to die. They have different methods. We have arrived at your final steps. We should never have had to get here. You have misbehaved. Now you have the consequences. We will tell you how."

They showed me a film of Hank carrying things for me, fixing things, guarding, advising me. It was like a propaganda film of Hitler. In real life, Hank then came to my house and helped me put together IKEA furniture. Their preplanned help validated their mind control film. They use ordinary life to substantiate mind control programs.

1. Destroy the relationship with Alison

"The rage you feel towards me and Liz, you will put on Alison. Alison gave you to us. One word from her and you would have remembered who we are. She was duped because she wanted to be duped. Transfer your rage to her. She deserves it."

The supervisor Carl strutted into the building's basement. Appearances like that are always scripted. "Is this the little slut?"

Liz: "It is she."

Carl: "Make sure the bond is broken between her and Alison the whore. Don't let her go there again. Isolate her. Let her get so lonely, she breaks. She'll come back to us, the fart. We'll make her into a little Nazi yet. Heil Hitler." They saluted one another Nazi-style.

Another time, Liz and her husband carried me screaming from the sliding door in their home: "Gag her," Liz said and Jeff stuffed a knotted rag in my mouth. I wouldn't walk. "Carry her," Liz said. Jeff, who had a rotator cuff tear, said, "It will tear my shoulder." "Who cares about your shoulder?" she said. Jeff flung me over his shoulder so that my head hung around his backside. "Knock her out." A rag of drugs went over my face.

Liz: "Watch her foot. We don't want any bruises." Bruises can evoke memory.

In the basement black chair:

Liz: "Alison is your enemy. She's like Ann. There's no difference between Alison and Ann. She dumped you. Why would you be here with us if Alison was your friend? You'll never get away from us. You're better off with us. Give up. You'll never escape. Everyone is against you. You must never see the witch Alison again. If you ever see her, we will skin her alive. It would be good riddance to her and her kind."

Hank: "Take it easy, Liz."

They must have been trying out a new method of interrupted programming. They would give one of the usual kinds of commands with some kind of torture such as sexual or injecting or pretending to inject diseases, then make me unconscious for a short time by placing a cloth drenched in chloroform over my face. When I woke up, they would repeat this sequence with a different torture and command. It lasted all night.

Another torture they used was injecting or pretending to inject chemical hormones of the opposite gender.

They said my therapy was a waste, but I knew my therapy had not been a waste for I had worked through the major part of my mind control. I would not have been able to reach in so deeply without Alison's help and support. I would have died knowing nothing about myself.

2. Don't recognise them

While I was in their black chair, Liz showed me a picture of someone else and told me that is whom I saw and that I couldn't tell anyone's identity.

"This person [in the picture] is doing this to you. The imposter is hurting you, not the real me. You think you know us but you don't. You think I'm the real Liz but I'm not. Look at this picture. He is pretending to be Hank but he is not Hank. So you see you don't know who we are."

3. Use my psychic abilities on their behalf

Psychic acuity is what these cults desire the most. I don't know why they believe psychic murder works, or perhaps they are just playing.

They direct people with these alleged psychic powers to do their attempted killing for them because no evidence points back to the people who ordered the ineffective destruction.

Satanists did not want prayers, good feelings, and thoughts invading territories they believed to be dominated by evil and their own.

A board illustrated different parts of the world: Washington DC, New York, Chicago, Seattle, Florida, Hawaii, Victoria, Montreal, Paris, Hong Kong, Buenos Aires, all of Korea and China.

"These are the places you stay away from psychically. You block these places. I am the new Fuhrer of Chief Rain-in-the-Face. You will bow down to me."

A programmer showed me a photograph of an honest therapist who does not want to be identified and said "He is one of us but if you ever remember this, we will have to kill him and it will be your fault and that's another thing you will have on your head—all because of the memory work you and Alison had to do."

"Iphigenia, I want this nice man dead. Direct your power to killing him. Let's give him a heart attack, 1-2-3, in his office. You know where his office is. You are in the building across the street. You can practise on my mother-in-law. Shut up, Jeff."

"There are no safe therapists. As soon as we bump off Alison, there will be none."

They talked about psychic killing or killing with the mind, not killing in person. I didn't believe this program as it went in. The photo didn't look like him. They said he was one of them, and they usually don't threaten to kill their own.

4. Housework

Liz: "You will buy all the food. You will clean the house and do the laundry. The living room windows could use a cleaning."

I ask inside my brain, who followed these orders?

I answer, children who watch over the infants.

Why didn't anyone run away after the first time?

We didn't know how to run away and no one else knew what was happening.

Children who watch over the infants, why didn't you tell someone who knew how to run away?

Four year old: Max created us. He said we aren't allowed to talk to anyone else or he would kill that person the way he killed my Daniel. We worried they would kill Alison.

I answer, if you talk to others in your inside world, it will only make Alison safer. The danger is in our not knowing what's happening. Maybe that's too hard to understand.

Four year old: I've seen more of life than you have. Daniel also left me to bad people.

Are there other small caves in the cave left in my internal brain landscape? Are there other sections? May I please at least have the dignity to know what's happening to me?

5. Where to live and whom to be friends with

They have established communities of satanists.

Liz: "Why can't she do what I say? I told her to go to Cabaro Beach. Why can't she just listen?"

Carl: "There's too much resistance. It's not worth the fight."

Liz: "Then where should we send her? I refuse to drive more than two hours and I like the beach there."

Carl: "Hank doesn't have the time to travel much for this. How many puppets is he in charge of now? Seventy-five, 150?"

Liz: "Many more."

Carl: "Boulspo. Do we have enough people there?"

Liz: "I don't know. Probably."

Carl: "There's Port Saints."

Liz: "That's too far. Though I'd like to see her in a grubby little town like that."

Carl: "Port Saints is loaded. Let's send her there."

Liz: "I'm always being inconvenienced."

Who in me recorded this conversation? I ask myself.

One of the soldiers, someone inside says.

Why didn't you move to Port Saints?

I didn't like it there. I had looked at the town, small city, and psychically saw a thin layer of black dust, like a residue from evil. I was afraid to disobey them and went instead to a nearby very slightly cleaner town.

Who's answering me now?

Soldiers, then psychics.

Why didn't you run away?

People inside couldn't run—I don't know why—and we couldn't abandon them.

They are not really people inside. They are more like thought waves that became paralysed in time. They are what the perpetrators think of as "puppets".

Maybe I'll have fewer problems in a new place, provided they didn't make me go there, I thought.

Carl: "Let's get her to the black chair and seal this with suicide programming."

Liz: "Bitch."

After they ordered a part of me where to live, they told me which friends to have:

Hank: "Lonely girl, lonely girl, where are you?

Lonely girl, lonely girl, what's to do?

Lonely girl, lonely girl, we can kill you.

Lonely girl, lonely girl, where are you?"

"We're going to send you friends because you're so lonely and they will take care of you, and you can be part of that group and you won't be lonely any more, and you'll never get out of the cave and you'll never swim up the Red River. So play in the mud, lonely girl, but you'll never swim up the Red River."

This part curled smaller and smaller and slipped under my vertebrae. The Red River is an internal pathway that makes my mind control cohesive. It is a lid placed over the mind control system.

Liz: "I'll be your friend, Wendy."

When I left the "safe house" and moved to Prim, Liz said, "We had to give up some privacy but I made a friend," implying that she and I had become friends. Every single word out of these people is programming.

When I finally told Alison, she asked, "Where did Lonely Girl originate? Age?"

"Four and a half."

"How many Lonely Girls are there?"

"150."

"How many in the cave?"

"Just one. He tried to get five but the older ones ran away."

Alison continued, "Originally, how were you all made? Were you made? Did you make yourselves?"

"We were made at four and a half, in the basement of Pleasant Hills after Daniel had just been murdered. They said I would always be lonely, looking for someone, and I would never find love again. My uncle sang the lonely girl song to the tune of 'When you wish upon a star' and then blew into a recorder with the tune."

For my last session in Chief Rain-in-the-Face, a team of programmers and an electricity expert assembled in the electric shock room in the office building basement. They must have called out Lonely Girl.

Programmer: "You will go to the Chinese restaurant, Fortune Star, on Christmas Day with the synagogue. You will see the dinner advertised in the newspaper. You will take the seat left empty for you. You will arrive ten minutes late so that you know where to sit. You will talk with the woman sitting opposite you. Her name is Brenda. [Aside: Tighten the head vice.] You will report to her. She will be your temporary escort and confidante. [Another dose. She's waking. Another dose.] Tomorrow you will leave our care. You will have new enforcers. You will never suspect them as being ours. If you ever don't obey, you will be punished. We won't kill you but we would make you suffer more than you can ever imagine."

Hank: "She'll leave tomorrow. She's in Prim not Port Saints, but it doesn't matter that much."

Programmer: "Well, she's out of my hair now."

Hank slipped him cash—a pile of hundred dollar bills. The chauffeur drove back to Liz's house.

November 18, 2014, right before I left:

Carl: "We are angry that you didn't buy a house on Cabero Beach. We have taken over that area. Now you will have to be punished. The first month after you move to Prim, you will kill yourself. You can hang yourself or take your pills. You are our toy. But we want you dead now. You have become useless. Some queen. Your life is no longer protected. You comply or we will kill Alison and your dog. You are a disgusting traitor."

Humiliations:

Good self-esteem loosens and repels mind control. Therefore programmers repeatedly make surviving victims feel bad about themselves. They direct these humiliations to very young parts who believe what even bad adults say.

Hank: "You're ugly. No one will want to look at you. You belong only with us. You will do what we say. If you don't do what we say, then we will drop bombs on the whole world. Many will die if you don't obey."

Liz: "You are so filthy, disgusting, ugly. This is the only place in the world you could ever be accepted. You're too ugly to live. Look, the two sides of her face are so different. Hank, could you even them out? Maybe punch here. No, it's still lopsided. Jeff, punch there."

(Here Liz had summoned three year old parts in me whose cheekbone had been broken. They build new trauma on past traumas. No wonder I have such problems with my jaw and ear now, I think.)

Liz: "Of course, you'll never be beautiful like me. But now you at least look a little more even.

"By the way, the shower needs cleaning."

The evil was palpable in the room and on their skin.

Programmers sometimes lose control of themselves, say things that aren't permitted.

While in Liz's home, Liz beat me with her red bat. Jeff remained asleep in their bedroom. Iris, her mother, stayed downstairs in her apartment.

As Liz pounded on my back, she screamed in her tight, angry voice:

"You will never go back to Alison's.

You will never go to another conference.

You will never write another book.

You will never have more memories.

You will never disobey us again."

She showed me a playing card with the picture of a geometric queen. "This is you and you are destroying us." She ripped up the card into little pieces and hit my head with her bat, especially on my ear. Iris wobbled up from downstairs.

"Lizzy, Lizzy," she said. Liz, who may or may not have had her hearing aid in, turned sharply and struck her frail mother. Iris fell down.

Jeff eventually came out of the bedroom. He wore clothes so he must have taken the time to dress. Even though he was afraid of Liz, he finally pulled her into her bedroom and locked the door from the outside.

The scene reminded me of my mother beating me and my father slowly coming to pull her off. She had destroyed my hearing in one ear. They set the stage early in your life and attempt to build upon it as long as they can.

Jeff told Iris, who was bleeding, that he was taking her to the hospital. He put a drug-cloth over me, dragged me to my bed, injected me.

Jeff: "You will sleep and in the morning have tea and toast."

Hurt and angry, a sliver in me jumped out of my evoked part and combined my parents' betrayal and Alison's bringing Liz, Hank, and Carl into my life.

All my evoked parts went back to sleep in their internal nooks. In the morning, I had tea and toast and remembered nothing.

During this time, a local government office gave Liz an award for doing extra-good community protection. Her family and I attended the ceremony.

DOWNTOWN CHIEF RAIN-IN-THE-FACE

They have to correct immediately any mishap that occurs during programming. Either Liz or Jeff must have reported Liz's blunder—that she said I was destroying them—or possibly they placed Iris in a trance and she reported.

Hank the fixer called out young tortured ones and my major queen personalities. He showed me the tarot card of the upside down hanged man, did hand signals, and strangled me to make me feel more powerless.

Hank: "You are not destroying us. You are nothing, a worm who crawls on soil, a rat in the gutter, a pauper, not a princess."

"Come out and listen carefully, slut, bitch, imbecile, whore." (They often use four nouns in a row to insult.)

Programmers and my mother started calling me a whore when I was four years old.

Hank shook me. Torture victims came out. He lit a cigarette lighter, which was supposed to call out the three burnt infants, but the original Illuminati queen Philomena in me blocked it. He couldn't tell. If the new programmers are not psychic or even intuitive, and most probably aren't, their kingdom will fail. He showed me Liz's red bat and tried to blot out all memory.

"You never saw this." He held up the queen card, the same kind Liz ripped. "You never saw this. Liz is your friend. She loves you. She is giving you a warm, safe, temporary home. She is a safe, caring person. That's why Alison sent you here to be cared for." Here they contradicted themselves. First they said Alison meant to hurt me by sending me to them. Then they said Liz is wonderful. In addition, they often say different things to different parts inside their victims' brains. Even one slip can make mind control crumble if other listening parts register the misinformation.

After every statement, there was stronger-than-usual electricity.

"Iris has medical problems. She's old and ready to die. Liz would never hurt her mother. She does everything for her mother. Your head doesn't hurt. You never had a concussion."

"Your hearing is fine. No problems."

Hank gave me hand signals to remember nothing, drugged me, and drove me back to Liz's prison.

As I remembered three years after this occurred, my back hurt and I had a headache. How strong body memories can be even years later. Many experience body memories decades later. As electricity and drug barriers disintegrated in me, running patterns and the feel of shoe laces being tied in my brain began.

Should I be abducted again, I hope I can remain aware in the moment.

When I was four or five, some time after Daniel died, I went to the corner of 108th Street and 68th Road, held my palms out and looked up to the hazy dark sky and said, "God, there must be a place for me, please send me to an orphanage or some-where, somewhere where I will be loved and not hurt."

My early programmers probably told me to go to that corner and ask God for help so that they could show me how God doesn't listen, and so that during the ritual that night, I would hear God laugh at me from the skies. But even though I was told to pray like that, my feelings were real. I was at that corner again, not knowing which way to turn.

Two bees banged against the windows. The door to Liz's patio was open but they could not retrace their path. They crashed again against the glass. I did not associate what was happening to me. All I had to do was fit what I could in the trunk of my car, wait until they both went to work and drive east. Far east. Anywhere east. My outside parts felt the desire to get away. I had become very depressed. The few inside parts who knew what had happened to me in Chief Rain-in-the-Face must have been rumbling inside about finding a way to flee. I told Alison on the phone that I wanted to drive east. Not knowing what was happening to me in the "safe house," she thought I was acting on a program to return to New York and discouraged me. I didn't leave and followed their orders to stay in the area. Those inside parts didn't push through. I didn't become aware of what was happening to me. The bees fell to the ground.

Noise is oppressive in Chief Rain-in-the-Face.

EXERCISES FOR SURVIVING VICTIMS

If you are a survivor or surviving victim, are you afraid someone helping you will be hurt because you are trying to break free? If so, raise the question with your helpers so that they can make their own choices. You cannot sacrifice your own healing to protect someone who doesn't even know you are doing so.

Encourage your hidden parts to speak about fears and anger. Try to pinpoint any feeling within yourself that points to betrayals. Some emotions can lead you to that truth. Betrayals can be as plentiful as leaves on trees.

Did anyone say things to you with the purpose of making you feel bad about yourself? Why do you think they wanted to do this? What did they say?

Are you overly sensitive about the smell of your bowels? How do you account for this sensitivity?

Does your head frequently jerk or shake seemingly spontaneously? How do you account for this body reaction? Could a mind control device have created this response in you?

Keep asking inside until you feel certain about whether you still have perpetrators in your life.

If you do, go into self-protection mode:

Inform many people of the identities of those who are accessing you. Put it in writing.

Get an alarm system if you can afford one.

If possible avoid going out at night. Abductions also take place in daylight, so be careful where you walk, especially if you are walking alone.

Keep looking for parts within that may not know what is happening to them and gently try to enlighten them.

If the area you are living in is infested with mind controlled satanists, consider moving somewhere else, though that carries its own dangers. If you do move, make sure that none of your parts tell anyone where. Consider whether it is better to stay put and fight.

Ask your inside world if anyone instructed you to live where you live. Investigate among your parts why you live where you do. Neighbours who move in after you may not be innocent.

If you are a helper, keep telling the person you are helping not to protect you. Some surviving victims will sacrifice themselves to protect others. If victims give in to perpetrators' threats, it is difficult for them to make progress. It at least slows recovery down and their idle threats are used only to scare.

PRIM, WA

I bought an apartment in a condominium I didn't like or want in Prim, Washington. That is not its real name because this is not about disparaging one particular city. It is about spotlighting the kind of treachery that takes place in many tiny and large cities and rural towns across the world. I lived in Prim for over two years and busied myself with decorating and looking for interesting activities. After a few weeks of distractions, I became lonely. I hadn't realised that sudden strong feelings point to programming.

Christmas dinner

Liz telephoned me: "I am keeping tabs on you, Princess Wendy. Go to the Christmas dinner at the Chinese restaurant with the synagogue, you Jew-bitch."

She must have summoned a child part since she referred to me as princess. Since this was a Nazi section, there was anti-Semitism. This call was around December 10, three weeks after I moved to Prim. That was about the time I suddenly became lonely. Without the mind control, I would not have felt lonely. I had been feeling relieved to be away from these perpetrators. Those who have been tortured from birth have trouble

67

living in close quarters with others, and anyone has trouble living with vicious, intrusive people.

Controllers place a cloth soaked in chloroform over victims' faces which makes them unconscious for a short time, and give them an injection whose effect lasts much longer. Drugs erase memory, weaken the victim's will, and allow a section or piece of the brain to be isolated. Electricity builds substantial walls around the isolated section that will contain a specific part with triggers to bring it out, with taught commands and instructions.

Most programming sessions involve victims being tied up, having a head vice tightened continuously, being electric shocked or tasered, and having guns held to them. Perpetrators also threaten and beat victims. I won't keep repeating these torture measures, but they are central to most official mind control procedures.

They came to my new house.

Hank: "This is to make sure you're going to that Christmas dinner. Or we'll have to go to the trouble of killing your friend and her dog."

"You're lonely. You need friends. Remember how lonely you are. How sad. Poor Wendy. You'll go to the dinner and make a friend."

"Your new contact and leader is Rachel Marks. You will do whatever she says. You will obey her or you will be punished."

My heart broke further and the sting of my awareness of betrayals rose. There are two awarenesses: the one during the abuse and the one during the memory process.

My heart exudes despair and spits out grief like a thick syrup. All this pain is who I am. Go ahead, lungs. Keep expelling.

After the Christmas dinner, Brenda first introduced me to Rachel, who brought in her team. Their network of writer-satanists, unwilling slaves mostly, flowed into my life to entrap me, though I thought at the time to offer friendship. Now we could write together some mornings, and some nights the same people could torture me. There must be quite a few satanists in Prim and Port Saints for there to have been a large group of writers/victims-perpetrators. How arrogant and naïve of me to think that new friends come that easily. How blind I was not to have known they were fellow-surviving-victims. The torture was less intense than in Chief Rain-in-the Face, and the perpetrators somewhat less vicious. The big wheels who flew to Victoria from the East and West Coasts did not bother with Prim.

Their first agenda was to prevent me from returning for therapy to Victoria.

These memories emerged reluctantly. I had to struggle. Any bilateral movement such as walking and swimming helped flush them out. I went for a swim. The memory came out on the ninth return length.

In late 2014, my perpetrators, Hank and his wife Rose put my furniture together and continued their masquerade. Rose held down my shoulders after Hank banged my head and strangled the drugged me. They take you to the brink of death to put in commands.

"Don't ever go back there. Don't ever go back there or I will kill your dog. You're not to see her again. You're not to remember this."

Rose (in an exaggerated Southern accent): "Give it to her good, hon." She said that repeatedly as Hank pressed on my Adam's apple. I became mist and had no body.

After they finished, at my front door, he said, "At least you got some furniture out of it." Perhaps he wanted me to be grateful.

He broke a barrier. He hinted that I got something and lost something. Any implication can cut through electricity and drugs and bring out the inside kernel that holds the truth. That is one reason why surviving victims and their therapists writing books and giving presentations are important. The information and message can pierce mind control and the frozen tension of amnesia, especially if victims want to know.

During this memory sequence, when I got out of the pool, I looked back to where I swam and saw my body or essence in the water—so intense is remembering.

From the location of the pain in my heart, I could trace which part or personality was out. This heartbreak was coming high up in my heart, from three infant personalities. "I thought I wasn't going to be hurt anymore," they said.

During a break-in to my home:

Liz with a knife at my dog's throat: "You will always answer to 'filthy, dirty bitch-witch' or we're on our way to Victoria to kill your Alison.

"We can get you to do whatever we want right under Alison's nose and she wouldn't know. She doesn't care enough about you to pay attention. She just cares about herself and her children."

Hank used the key to lock my door from the outside. He didn't want the bolt left unlocked, which could jog my memory.

These perpetrators didn't call out any parts that I had discovered and integrated during the course of my therapy. They called out parts created long ago and those that my more conscious mind didn't yet know about. For example, Mengele had created a secret chamber where he placed an eight and a ten year old.

"Why not nine years old?" his assistant asked.

"I don't like the number nine." Those are the people who take control of others' minds.

Mengele taught these internal children a pattern of taps. If I didn't learn it, he said he would cut my toes off. He repeated the pattern many times until it became ingrained. He created sleepwalkers who walk with their arms outstretched. Liz activated one of these parts who walked to the front door, even after an intruder opened it. The alarm went off. Hank held a gun to my temple. Jeff walked me to the alarm keypad in the cupboard and I had to shut it off or he'd kill me. Someone got hold of my dog. If I didn't shut the alarm off, they

70

would take her away. That is the one threat that was not idle. It would have been far too risky to approach a well known person like Alison. They left my dog alive to have something to hold over me. I might never have met these hidden personalities without break-ins. Every example I describe represents many occurrences.

To find the original holders of other commands, I had to go further into the Nazi and neo-Nazis section within me. Mengele had stolen some of Illuminati Max's black slaves and placed new commands in them. Unfortunately, hidden mind controlled parts are often too afraid to think rationally.

Programmers use pictures on cards and other images to seal in commands. One programmer may change the direction of how a card is held without informing anyone else or recording the move. Surviving victims are programmed one way, then the programming is usurped and changed so that the original programmer can no longer access it. They are fighting over control of victims' brains.

The first thief-programmers steal the child's brain. The second thief-programmers steal the program inserted in this child's stolen brain. The originator of the program may attempt to retrieve the program but may not guess that the thief-programmer changed the angle of the visual clue.

BOULSPO, 2016

Liz found it inconvenient to travel to torture me for she needed more time to shop and go to the hairdresser's. Instead, she summoned me to a town near her. She was late as usual. I waited in a pet shop that held an animal rescue. Two dogs had bonded. One was adopted. The other, heart-broken, forsaken, barked endlessly. When Liz finally arrived, we shopped and she bought for herself. I had no memories or realisations of her true identity at the time. A few hours later, I was ready to go home but she wanted to have dinner. What I hadn't remembered before was a gun suddenly in my side— one of her pink miniature girly guns. She has many. I couldn't understand why I went to that restaurant until I associated that she walked a part of me to a restaurant with the gun in my left ribs. Perpetrators walk you somewhere with focused purpose, urgently, like a rat in a maze. We ate as she kicked my shins under the table, another trigger. I'm supposed to always pay for her meals. Some of me must have been more healed then, because for the first time I didn't pay. Her face became blank, then troubled, then exasperated. Using hand signals, she walked me behind a building cluttered with rubbish bins. Hank appeared. No one else was there but this town is cult territory. He probably had guards watching in alleys. He showed me playing card triggers, punched me in the stomach, strangled me, kicked me in the groin. "Put the gun away, Liz. We don't need it now." The other piece of this memory that had been slow reaching the surface is that Liz complained about my not buying her dinner. Hank emptied my purse and gave my money to Liz, who put it in her bra.

When I couldn't breathe at all, Hank said, "Kneel over." He put a larger gun from his holster into my right temple. "I want to talk to Queen Iphigenia. I should kill you now. Maybe I'll take you to the warehouse first and skin you. I'll make a deal with you. You drive back to Prim now, stay there for the rest of your life and never return to Victoria or see Alison again and I'll leave you alone. Will you do that?"

Lightning, I became lightning striking them dead. "Yes," I said.

"One little sock to the ear [with the gun handle], one little sock to the jaw for old time's sake." Hank put his gun away, snapped his fingers and did hand gestures in front of my face before he dismissed me.

Of course, I returned to Victoria. Beating up clients who are in therapy is satanic cults' methodology. I wonder how many therapists don't see what is happening to their clients. I wonder how many clients right now aren't seeing or consciously feeling what is happening to them. They may feel the just administered pain but attribute it to something else like an illness or old injury acting up. Or the tortured parts may go deep inside and the more forward parts don't feel the pain. And I wonder if any external witness saw but is too afraid to tell. Terror wipes out other feelings.

It confuses me that I followed their commands to move to Prim and be in association with the "friends" but not to follow the fine points of their orders or be silenced. If I were rebellious, why not completely rebellious? Even when most of the brain is captured in a net and squeezed hard, slivers escape and act like their unhampered selves. Satanic professionals can't kill all of the mind.

74

My resistance goes back a long way. Even when I was a child, my programmer complained about my disobedience. Max disguised as Wiezenslowki: "Here you are everything. Everywhere else you are nothing. Here you are queen. Everywhere else you are a nothing. Here you are a genius. Everywhere else you are stupid. You belong to us. Why aren't you happy?"

(To my unhappy mother): "Why isn't she happy? What is the matter with her? Everyone else is happy."

The issue became to live without a body and mind or to live without a soul. Satanism is soul abuse. Remembering and then discovering who you are begins the repair of the soul.

With no escape possible as a child, I became a white witch.

JUDAISM AND ANTI-SEMITISM

S atanism doesn't believe in God, but programmers use religion in their programming. One example is victims are told they will please Jesus by obeying their mind control commands.

Being from New York, I hadn't experienced much anti-Semitism in my surface life. In an Ohio college was the first time I noticed it. The Christian mother of a college friend thought Jewish people had horns. Perhaps my friend did too. In under life, Nazi groups used Judaism in their programming. Like those usurping Christian messages, most programmers and relatives tried to make me feel guilty about not keeping their secrets. Decades later, on the West Coast, my torturers expressed that kind of hatred and self-hatred.

The anti-Judaism method was used in my past programmed life:

Parent: "No one must know about us. If you tell, there will be another Holocaust and then your mother and father will be killed and it will be your fault."

The infamous Dr Cameron in Canada: "Filthy Jew. Another filthy Jew. Talk and you will all be put back in the ovens."

A psychiatrist-programmer: "Filthy disgusting Jew. If you ever remember, you will all be incinerated and good riddance. What a bitch."

The New York Jewish psychologist-programmer: "Wendy, if you talk, you will hurt us all."

An official programmer/witch: "Jesus-haters. You will be wiped out."

A therapist-programmer: "You're all disgusting rats. You belong in the ovens."

A Baltimore Orthodox Jewish programmer: "If you ever talk about our community, you will make the Jews a pile of ash."

An Asian programmer: "Do you want to cause another Holocaust?"

One of the Prim Jewish "friends": "If you talk, you will destroy our community. We will all go to concentration camps. It will be your fault if the world hates us again."

It surprises me that it took me years not to succumb to that worry. It's as if my brain is filled with algae rising to the surface of a dirty ocean. My thoughts and memories are delayed. My mind struggles. The sting of my awareness of betrayal travels further in.

A FAVOURITE PLACE TO WALK IN PRIM

I tried to make a little life for myself as a quasi-integrated person who didn't know about the abuse my body and personalities inside me suffered. I found a favourite place to walk by the water. My dog could be off leash. It was dangerous for small dogs only when the parent and newborn eagles perched high on towering trees. I hadn't realised it was dangerous for me too.

Salmon spawn in this dyke. I walked absorbing the flow of the waters surrounded by alders, magnificent stones and rocks along the cliffs, and farmland oozing with vitality. It was my haven where I could be part of nature. Until two men jumped out from close to the water. With a gun, they walked me to the parking lot, shoved me in a car, and drove to nearby Port Saints as my heart stopped and raced. My skin stood up. They parked in the back and dragged me down several concrete steps that led to the basement of a chain motel called (I'm making up names) the Black Leopard. In a not up-to-date black chair, with a head vice and brackets for ankles attached, others began.

"Friend" Brenda: "Should we bump her off?"

Another assistant: "No. What for?"

Brenda: "She's too much trouble and dangerous." I had begun to suspect something about the head of the coven and spoke to people about it. Satanists cherish their secrecy and cannot tolerate any whispers of truth leaking.

Christina brought in food. These liked to eat as they tortured.

Brenda: "It's going to be a long night."

They tried to evoke parts who had watched my mother feed my sister and starve me. It is good to learn that my mother did not starve me on purpose but was ordered to do so. I am happy for her. They also wanted me to think this episode of torture would not be short-lived but would go on for hours.

It must have been 4 or 5 p.m. Brenda sat in a chair pontificating:

"We want you to stop saying bad things about Rachel. I hope you agree. Christina, bring in a doll. I would hate to have to burn this doll. You're probably wondering where Blossom is. Our guys brought her home to your house. We would hate to hurt her or worse, of course. So it's important that you agree and cooperate."

Some internal parts responded right away to the trigger of the burnt doll. But the rest of me wondered why a burnt doll would elicit such a response. It was a doll, not a person.

The trigger shoved me into guilt-despair. Drugs increased anxiety.

It took some delving to find the parts who had been surrounded with burnt dolls and who felt responsible for loved ones, and had terribly low self-esteem. I found an infant, five year old, and queen parts. Programmers from both the Nazi and Illuminati had said:

"These are your children. You destroyed your children. You are a bad mother. You are a murderer."

Why did I think it was my fault when they threatened to kill Alison?

These coven leaders bask in sterling reputations built on lies.

She showed me triggers from a deck of playing cards. "Queen Philomena, you think you are high and mighty.

Your mother called you high-handed. You say another bad word about our queen Rachel and you, the doll, and the dog are dead, burnt meat."

After I was dumped off at home, I slept for a long time and remembered nothing.

When I woke, I walked along the halls of my house. The walls became a blur. I had become vapour coating faraway walls with fur. I was far away from myself and didn't even know something bad had happened. Only hours had passed. Why was my dog wagging her tail furiously? Why was she so happy to see me? I knew my body hurt. Even my ankles felt raw and scratched. I stalked the halls. My heart went wild. Why was I having a crisis at 3 a.m.? Why was my stomach howling? Hadn't I eaten dinner? My head filled with dizzying confusion. I had hours of blank spots. I couldn't put anything together. They must have perfected their cocktails of drugs to cause complete amnesia. I remained a burnt, empty carcass. Until I remembered.

Years later, I stood on an old wooden bridge overlooking a waterfall in another part of the country. Three young men approached. I thought they would throw me over onto rocks. They passed by, chatting and joking. Trauma sticks.

A decade before, I had spent years in New York City choreographing and doing performance art—a time when I felt close to myself—all while being mind controlled. My enemies did all they could to stop me from being myself. People get used to being amnesiac and living double lives. From birth on we were trained for that kind of duality of existence.

DOG SITTING

If paid perpetrators can get you to clean their house and pay for their food, they can also get you to dog sit. If they want to go to a wedding and can get you to dog sit in their house, they might as well have other torturers work you over while you are there. They can split the payment money. While I lived in Prim, I drove back to Chief Rain-in-the-Face. Because my tortured parts did not communicate with my unknowing personalities, I could not protect myself. I asked myself internally for months if something I didn't remember had happened when I dog-sat for Liz.

I had been asleep when Liz's brother and his wife, family Nazis, came into Liz's house. They woke me and called out other hidden parts of me that hadn't come to the surface yet. The brother showed me a brick and a large naked doll. "Come out, Baby Big." Baby Big didn't come out because they didn't show me the complete sets of cue cards. Either they hadn't read my information book or it had not been recorded. It is possible that directions were recorded only in the Illuminati information book and that Nazis didn't have access to it. What he didn't know is that my original childhood master programmer had turned the card showing a crow upside down and side-ways. When I was a child, Max said:

"You have to be pinched, shown a brick and the doll and the crow in these positions, Baby Big, to come out. Otherwise you remain underneath the pelvic bone hidden from view." Liz's brother had pinched my arms and legs and left rows of bruises, but Baby Big did not come out and he didn't realise it.

The brother: "You're going to die, Baby Big, and you're going to do it to yourself when you're back in Prim, you filthy dirty Jew."

In Liz's house, the parts that slid to the surface didn't know what Liz's brother was talking about.

Sister-in-law: "Beat her up. Not in the head. Don't leave marks."

He hit me in my right hip especially. Liz's brother pulled up my nightgown and unzipped his fly. The wife said, "What are you doing?" The brother said, "I'm going to rape this bitch and shred her." I disappeared underground, coiled into a snail. The rest of me was nowhere.

Wife: "No you're not." She hit him with the brick, leaving a trail of blood—little spots in a row on the hall carpet.

The sister-in-law prepared a needle. "I'm giving her the miracle drug. She'll never remember." I fell into a coma-sleep and remembered nothing.

The severe depression I had been experiencing is in these surrounding parts but not in the one they tried to call out. These surrounding parts believe there is no reason anymore to be alive and have no belief in mankind. They think of them-selves as just a slave who doesn't even know she is a slave. I heard the front door close.

Memories are not erased forever. A year and a half after this dog sitting episode occurred, the trail of blood spots on the carpet reached my consciousness. I had scrubbed those spots thinking that perhaps my dog had shed blood, and I didn't want to stain Liz's carpet. Yes, I am an idiot. Doing nice things for torturers was a theme of my life then.

THE LOCALS WANTED ME OUT OF PRIM

The people, especially the coven leader, who were forced to befriend me and who must have been punished for my partial disobedience wanted me out of their territory, and were willing to give up their pay for it.

Rachel: "You will leave this community. We don't want you here. Don't write any more of your stinking books. Bringing trouble to us. You fucking maniac. Get out of here. We don't want you here, you and your stinking books. You'll never write another book. You dirty, filthy Jew."

Cult victims often go along with their perpetrators thinking something worse will happen if they don't cooperate, but worse things happen when they do cooperate. Those low down on the hierarchical scale and in the middle range can be set up to take the blame for satanic crimes.

Rachel, her assistant Elaine, and others streamed into my home. Hank commanded that if they went too far and I died, Rachel and Elaine would remain in the house to take the blame. In addition to the usual torture, morbidly obese Rachel used her weight as a weapon and sat on me while Hank gave commands. Bouncing on me, Rachel said, "Slave Girl, Slave Girl. You must obey. Don't talk about your books, don't talk about the whole thing, silence, Slave Girl."

"They told us to kill you and then stay here because they want to blame it on us. We won't do it only because we don't want to go to jail, not because we like you."

Elaine: "We're supposed to strangle you which would be easy because of your skinny neck. Everyone talks about your skinny neck."

Rachel: "So I guess you're lucky, for now anyway."

I dived deep into a swimming pool that wasn't there and crawled on its floor pretending it was the ocean.

They had made Rachel a big fish in this little pond of a rural coven, and the other perpetrator wealthy, but their commanders were happy to sacrifice them too. We are all stooges in this satanic world of theirs. Or they may have lied.

RETIREMENT COMMUNITIES

Satanists have retirement communities where used-up members go to live among their own in a reserve-type army. They need one another to make sure their amnesiac barriers don't dissolve over time. Being with normal people and not having their mind control tweaked recurrently could trigger awareness. The leaders know that coming from this background, they don't fit into the ordinary way of life even though some have jobs in the outside world. Some even have ordinary-life spouses. These retired satanists have their country homes and gardens to distract them from any internal searching. It's only the ones who try to escape and achieve freedom who live in isolation. That may change in time, as society becomes aware.

My ordinary life and integrated parts thought this coven leader was just obtuse and afraid. I didn't know her efforts came from programming, and that she had been forced to be oppressive. Perhaps it was after they made Rachel and Elaine into stooges that Rachel's child parts came further forward, and her theme turned from silencing to getting me to leave. She may have realised that my presence and disobedience hurt her reputation and might cost her her life. They probably didn't have these problems and instructions before I was ordered to live among them. I don't know the real reason for her turn. There may be a whole other under-story. The leaders may have ordered the change, though that doesn't make sense. It would have been easier for them to keep me in Prim and murder me there.

I had thought those "friends" liked me. I thought those nice things happened in life. I didn't know it was all phony, tricks, calculated. I didn't know that my life was a mask.

I think it's safe to assume that every time I was with these perpetrators, that I was torture-programmed. They called the beatings "encouragements".

By the end of my confinement in Prim, if I met interesting people, I didn't follow through. I was afraid to trust.

ALASKA

Alison presented on mind control in Alaska. I went thinking it might be the only time I could attend her workshop. I drove from Prim, and Liz drove me to the airport in Chief Rain-in-the-Face. We arranged for her to pick me up late in the afternoon when I returned a few days later. I left my keys in her glove compartment. When I arrived back in the airport, I planned to sit with Alison and keep her company for the long wait until her plane left for Victoria.

Liz arrived at the airport and called me long before she was supposed to pick me up, telling me where she was waiting. I must have been almost co-conscious because as I hugged Alison goodbye, leaving hours before I had planned, I wondered why Alison wasn't doing or saying something to stop me, which would have brought me to awareness then. Being co-conscious and even integrated in one section doesn't create co-consciousness in another section of the mind controlled, frozen brain. I reached co-consciousness a few months later anyway as the memories broke loose from their electric fences.

In the car, driving away from the airport, Liz attempted to call forth a specific personality, insisted I go into her mother-in-law's house to say hello, and called her husband to join us. He asked me if my plane was late, which seemed peculiar. They talked for about ten minutes, all of them sitting on sofas, the image of a perfect family happily together, the grandmother particularly pleased and smiling. I said I had to leave, thinking of the long drive home on isolated roads. When I came out of the bathroom, they tackled me.

The mother-in-law, her curved back bent all the way over, balancing on a walker, said, "Leave that precious woman alone."

My tackled parts jumped in a barrel and from its inside rolled it over a cliff.

Meanwhile a brave surviving victim in Alaska told her therapist about being assaulted by Celine, a visiting presenter, a supposedly healed victim, and the therapist told Alison. Liz had arranged for this same presenter to go to Alaska. The fragments of my mind started to meander together.

In the hall outside the bathroom, Liz screamed at me, "You harlot, you whore. Your harlot-whore-freak therapist got Celine in trouble. That bitch, that shrew of a piece of shit talked. [She meant the attacked surviving victim.] We'll take care of her and your quack. We'll get them. We got you."

Liz whispered to her husband, "Something's slipping." (I wasn't supposed to hear that.)

Liz was right. Something was slipping. It would take another year before I achieved full recognition of what had happened and who they were. But the exodus had begun. I had already joined the front people with the inside ones in the Illuminati section, and now the same thing had just begun to happen in the Nazi section of my battered brain.

Each section of the mutilated brain has its own gulf between the two captured armies. Surviving victims have to fill in each trench for there to be healing. Some of the original personalities may have been stolen and placed in other sections of the trespassed brain. Healing victims need to find those too.

One of the main necessary conditions of successful mind control and programmed amnesia is the separation of ordinary life parts (front people) from inside personalities who are trained to function in criminal ways. It is easier to help the inside parts communicate with one another internally than to leap the toxic barrier that divides the ordinary life from the more hidden secret one. These two divisions were not allowed to communicate. The division is as great as it is between people who grew up normally and those who were born into satanic cults. Two essentials of recovery are knowing which personality holds the specific information, and having the front people aware of what has happened in your life.

The separation between front people and inside ones is the most fraught joint of mind control. Perpetrators put fantasised internal gulfs, ditches, seas, any kind of electrified separation between the two sets of personalities. If you are a surviving victim of mind control, start early trying to persuade anyone from either side of the barrier to reach out to the other. When they reach out, they will be disobeying all the implanted mind control teachings and commands. Every system has rebels and brave ones. When they reach out to one another, they have cemented the start of their healing. Even if they are trapped or hunted or caught, they have still begun. Controllers will attempt to erase this inner knowledge, but if you reached out once, you can do it again. If you are caught again, perpetrators will place thick barriers between parts talking among themselves in your inside sections and even thicker barriers between the inside functioning parts and the parts living ordinary life. If you dissolved barriers once, you can do it again. You can match and surpass their perseverance. You can be free.

Yet most victims remain intimidated and terrified enough not to try to undo their mind control and escape. Moreover, satanists destroy their victims' identities and self-worth, which you need in order to tolerate change. Some surviving victims become complacent and do not try to escape. Is it not worth the temporary increased torture to find out who you are and what a real life is? Wouldn't it be worth anything to be able to live even for a little while as life was meant to be and no longer as a puppet of sick people's perverse experiments? They have taken away minds and bodies. Let surviving victims' souls lead them to freedom.

Still in the mother-in-law's house after the Chief Rain-in-the-Face airport, I had said I wanted to leave for home. Perpetrators like to turn things around and make commands. Liz and her husband: "We will run you off the road. You must drive off the road or we will kill Alison. Leave now."

All my parts raced to my car and drove towards Route 5 heading back to Prim. I turned left and they were not behind me, so I thought they might not follow me. After a pause, Liz, Jeff the husband, and Hank followed me in their car. Something in me must have been improving even though relevant information about these perpetrators hadn't yet penetrated my consciousness. The country roads have no lights. Their car came very close to mine on one of these isolated roads. I leaned on my horn, engaged my flashers, and did not drive off the tarmac. No one else was nearby, but they turned their car around. Your actions can stop perpetrators. You can be terrified and still act rationally. You can protect yourself. I made it home safely.

When I discovered this memory, I asked the parts telling me whether they were in or out of the glob, meaning my so far integrated mind. They said they went in the neo-Nazi section which is in the glob but I didn't yet know everything that had happened in this section.

If programmers cannot control you, they want you dead. But they can't take the chance of its looking like murder even though it is murder. They design the death to look like suicide. They were taking a chance with me because I am connected to two colleagues who would be able to guess what happened, Alison Miller and Neil Brick, and two knowledgeable friends, Philippa and Tim. I have also left lists of perpetrators to suspect and investigate with numerous people.

Shortly before I finally escaped from Prim:

Hank: "We don't want to kill you ourselves. We want you to do it. We want you to slit your wrists as your mother taught you—to draw trees on your arms. You don't have to do it tonight or even this month. You were already given a date, November 21, 2017. Do it then. One of the children who knows how to suicide, come out."

No one came out.

Hank: "Then I will make a new one in the here and now."

I couldn't stand the head pain, and something in me came out and said, "I will do it on November 21st." I don't remember saying that so it did not come from part of my integrated self. I felt suicidal on November 25th.

Like any diligent rememberer, I asked myself about the discrepancy in dates and the delay in the suicidal feeling. They must have had look-outs who saw me walking my dog on the 21st and 22nd. Hank and the supervisor returned to Prim. They opened my door with a key. Hank strangled me.

"You will take these pills the day after tomorrow." He left them on my bedside table. If the day after tomorrow was the 25th, then this would have happened on the 23rd.

Hank: "Should we kill the dog now or take it away?"

Supervisor: "I don't want to provoke her so much that she does something rash. She's too unpredictable."

THE START OF REMEMBERING

Satanists can torture too much. If a cup becomes overly full, it spills and memories slide out. Compulsive sadism boomerangs like any addiction.

Hearing this Alaskan surviving victim's story made some internal pieces of my brain face what had happened in Chief Rain-in-the-Face and tell the rest of me. That shock opened the next phase of my expedition to unification. Any signal, provocation, encouragement, or account of someone's life can allow an inside part to burst its barricades. It is no wonder then that satanists reprogram endlessly. They are afraid of victims' capabilities. This surviving victim also cautioned Alison that she was not safe. That information stimulated the parts deep inside me who were told my perpetrators would hurt Alison if I did not stop therapy. Those troubled parts deep inside began rising in me like dough in a warm kitchen. I remembered the local perpetrators in Victoria made an effigy of Alison. I began acknowledging consciously that to seek help may put others in danger. It is probable that the threats were idle, but my parts inside believed them at that time. At four years old, I had lost the only person who loved me. They told me it was because I loved him. They would have sacrificed him no matter what, but how can a four year old understand that kind of duplicity? An infected inside nerve did not want people to be hurt because of me. Try not to fall for their threats. It does no one any good. At least now I confronted this ungrounded dread that had allowed them to control me.

Electric shock paralyses and seals an impenetrable barrier around the section of the brain evoked to hold the memory. When that section of the brain is retrieved in recovery and its contents spilled, the section begins to come back to life. The brain flutters and spasms. The section is like a chick struggling to break its shell and emerge. Often programmers move a piece or slice of the memory sequence into a different part of the brain, sometimes far away from its original location, to make it difficult to put the whole memory together. When I got to that hidden piece, my mind felt like it was running a race in my brain.

My awareness of what had happened to me in Chief Rain-in-the Face started with the memory of my being dragged out of the back sliding door at Liz's house. Then the whole drama of my abuse unfolded, plus their getting their hands on me in Prim. This knowledge changed my life and even Alison's life, and even my two friends' lives, the ones who live in Victoria.

I wonder, what would have happened if I hadn't been incarcerated at Liz's? Would I have been safe?

The most horrible consequence was being deprived of the well-being and kindness of a regular life with people. Of trusting rather than being on guard. Of loving instead of hating. Being with good people is how you learn to be human. I have not known what life is supposed to offer. I have secret knowledge but have not experienced normal life.

If I was disobedient and also starting to realise who I am and what was still happening to me, then the abusers had to try other measures and bring in other perpetrators to stop me. While I was still in Prim, a lawyer they recommended to help me became my friend. I told her my story. She said she thought a detective she worked with might be able to give me guidance and help me escape. He came to my house and gave me tips on how to remain safe, none of which panned out. I wrote down everything he said on a yellow pad of paper. His presentation was smooth until he held up his iPhone like a prize fish he had just caught, dangled it in the air and recommended I buy one. By that time, everyone knew those phones are used to track people and it would be the worst thing to do if you want to hide. That was my clue, plus his denial that the phones could reveal locations. Surviving victims have to train themselves to listen to their inner alerts and to stop giving perpetrators the benefit of the doubt.

During this consultation, the table we sat at was by the sliding door to my patio. At first I hadn't remembered the detective gripping me, putting a cloth over my face and injecting my arm as he held other drugs under my nose. As I became unconscious, folded, and collapsed, I heard footsteps which must have been the lawyer's who entered and had not been there at the beginning.

Some familiar and unfamiliar external voices: "Is she out? Don't go back to Victoria. Stay here. We're in charge of you. We get money for you. We get plenty of money from you. We own you. We have to have you underfoot."

Lawyer: "She's going to drive away. She wants to escape us. She doesn't know where she's going."

Detective: "Put up roadblocks. She'll never get away from us.

Give her the injection." I felt large, rough hands pinch my forearm. "It's the amnesia drug. She'll remember nothing."

They called out starving, untouched, unloved infants in me and tortured and excoriated isolated five year olds.

"Make sure there's nothing left behind."

"Check for the rope, cards." I heard the sliding door open, close and I heard my groans. I felt three leaving through the back door and others leaving through the front door. There must have been escape cars parked in various directions. A good part of a coven must have been present.

When I came to, it was deep night. I found Blossom, let her out, and fed her. I noticed that I hadn't locked the sliding door and that the alarm was off, and I thought I was being careless again. I couldn't balance well. I saw the yellow pad of paper and the detective's card on the table. I remembered the interview. I ate cold cereal and milk. I slept again and remembered nothing except the interview. But drugs only cause amnesia temporarily.

I would like to kill, first tear apart limb by limb, organ by organ, all the people who hurt me there.

My life has been a lie. My relationships have been lies. I have been a false person.

Slowly I started packing and put my art supplies away. My last works are individual portraits of Alison, her dog, my childhood friend Daniel, and my friend Philippa. I thought I would never see them again.

I felt devastated, alone and afraid. I couldn't stop crying. I left Baltimore, I had a year in Victoria, now I had nothing again. My face was dissolving. When they came into my house, if I didn't shut the alarm off, they might have taken Blossom away.

TV shows had no meaning for me, but once in a while, one was about real betrayal. Then I could relate and feel that I wasn't the only one in the world.

All those times when someone offered friendship, invited me somewhere, seemed interested in me, they were mostly set-ups to have access to torture me and reinstate mind control.

"You'll never know who your friends are. You'll never know who your enemies are. You'll always be a slave, prisoner, whore, slut. You are a nothing, an abominable nothing," they said.

My heart feels slashed that all those "friends" in Prim turned out to be enemies who wanted to hurt me or worse.

Emotional pain can give birth to freedom.

A movement inside me began: parts tied with coarse rope, with head vices, those who hate these perpetrators, those who feel guilty about exposing Blossom to this appeared. My tears are so salty, they create furrows on my cheeks. I could use them to melt ice outside.

I think everyone inside my brain knows Alison meant no harm. But they all felt betrayed anyway. She didn't see and I couldn't talk. Why didn't I tell Alison I was being tortured? Perhaps children inside me were afraid of being sent away and I had no place to go. But who needs a therapist who sends you away? Or runs away? Even inside children don't. I was afraid of their murdering her. They followed me to Victoria. I had the responsibility to protect. I felt guilty. Why did I finally know then? I finally knew because I made my way to the other section where the information was. Until now I couldn't get through those electricity walls. It was not what therapists call resistance. I had not yet been positioned to access this information and these parts of my brain. Information melts electricity. As soon as I remembered, I told Alison. She wanted to know.

THE RESCUE

Even in grim lives, blessings may arrive. Friends, helpers. Someone who sees who you are, leads you to a crack in the enclosing impenetrable walls. A glint of sun, air comes your way, sometimes. I would not have known I existed had it not been for them. Kindness is in the world. And now tears burn instead of electricity searing my brain. Internal rock turns to sorrow with birth pains.

Surrounded by this nest of odious retired satanists and barely able to leave my home because it was unsafe, I didn't know what to do next. All I could think of was getting into my car and driving away. I had no idea where to go. My friend Philippa had been trying to persuade me to return to Victoria, but I was afraid of the local satanists who may find out that I was there and who might restart torturing me.

Just then, Alison called. She had just had lunch at Philippa's home. She said Philippa wanted me to live with her and her husband and spoke of community. In her home, under her care, I would be safe. My choice became driving off with only my dog to nowhere in particular or returning to dangerous territory. Alison had considerable influence over me, said it was the perfect solution. The three people in the world who cared about me would be together. That lured me. I chose love. *Deus ex machina* they entered my life, just as I was chanting to myself that I had to make my own decisions and trust only myself. Almost the next day, my friend Philippa alighted on this mess. I had had dental surgery the day before and was supposed to keep my blood pressure low. Instead we sorted, gave away, and stored my things all day and night. Philippa packed her car and mine to its gills. In sleep, my overtired body bobbed up and down on the mattress unable to rest. We left the next morning. The timing was terrible because of the surgery but also wonderful. She may have saved me from another night of torture. Perpetrators seek to prey on the sick and injured. I remained within Philippa's family nest and regained my health. There are people born into the normal world but willing to help others. They are rare but there. Victims are not completely alone, sometimes.

ALONE

In times of danger and uncertainty, people may revert to old ways. Newly coming out of mind control, I was unused to making decisions. During active mind control, I didn't feel the relinquishing of my mind. Later, when I finally got to know my abducted selves that had been, I stopped letting other people make decisions for me.

This time I stayed in Philippa and Tim's home rather than in a rental suite at the side of their house. Philippa is a natural mother and her husband Tim is a retired doctor and shepherd. He treats everyone as one of his sheep. I had never lived with people who cared about me before and had to adjust to living with kindness.

Alison and I had come together in a weird confluence of tracks and then parted. Shortly after I arrived back in Victoria, Alison said she was leaving to move far away and that I could not follow her. Alison is concerned for my safety and that my perpetrators will look for me where she is. But people decide for themselves how much danger they can tolerate.

She had been planning on retiring for years, even before I met her. With a primal need for family, she had left to be with them. Alison had worked in this field for decades and advanced the therapeutic study of mind control. She came to Philippa's house to say goodbye.

At the end of the visit I stood like Lot's wife by the road. Alison gave me a peripheral look of sorrow and told me to say goodbye to Jake, a dog I love, who was in the backseat of her new car. Jake's eyes stared at me through the window. His eyes held mine. I stared back at my anchor. Alison said goodbye in profile. Pain etched her face. I had already ended therapy with her, but she said I needed therapy and that she knew someone in Chicago. I stood, knees stiff, unable to move or not wanting to move. I remained a frozen pillar not turning but staring straight ahead through layers of agonies. She drove her sturdy car away. A child or naïve adult part in me must have popped out and thought perhaps she would come back. At the corner, she stopped with the indicator on, probably to clean her glasses or fiddle with one of the gadgets or look at the map. Hollow minutes passed. Then she made a right hand turn onto Widegate Road, and I knew I would never see the second most important person in my life again.

Every part of my brain that had ever been abandoned and tormented came out together in force. It takes a long time to come off that kind of rawness, perhaps two lifetimes.

When I moderated online surviving victims' discussion groups, I learned that many if not most felt abandoned. Being abandoned by therapists is one of its common themes. It is difficult to lose the only person who helps you know your story and still believes in you. Then all that is whisked away.

Grief is like a team of horses suddenly released into the wild. It is unstoppable.

A therapist touches infant parts as she finds them in hidden debris. Her heart touches their despairing heart. They are filled with shame but she thinks they are good enough. And that's what they get in life—someone who found them and whose heart touched theirs. Then that source of life leaves because she has her own real family, blood not water. My heart would begin churning as in eating itself alive.

106

There is a shortage of safe therapists in this field. Few people from the normal world can bear this heat for long. The small number of therapists drawn to this field burn out, get scared, discouraged, threatened, fatigued, or ill, give in to their families' objections, want something else, and/or cannot stand vicarious pain. Therapy is time-limited, not endless. All therapists grow old and eventually need to retire. It happens and the clients suffer unspeakably.

Honest therapists are often the link between two worlds. Some surviving victims have lost every one of their children, the rest of their families, and discovered that most of their friends were two-faced enemies. A therapist is usually the first person, aside from programmers and handlers, to speak with deeply inner parts. In discovery resides responsibility. And all while the minds of surviving victims and survivors realise that they have had a degrading life.

Therapists reach in and bring hidden away infants to the precipice of humanity. What happens when the therapist is no longer there? Without anyone who understands how to reach out to these, it may be harder for them to want to rejoin humanity. We are still in an age that does not believe that the world is run by the most evil people, and that infants' minds are tortured into pieces, and that children are trafficked and don't remember. Victims may be able to relate to the ordinary-society world as a false masked self, but not as a real self.

Some therapists can deal with their clients currently being tortured and others become too afraid. Some therapists have difficulty dealing with the specific intense feelings that precede or surround breakthroughs of memories. Then the client sometimes backs off from that feeling while in therapy.

And many are not safe therapists but pretend therapists sent to instil new programs in surviving victims' minds. Once those new programs are affixed, or old ones activated, their "superiors" take them off the job. Victims don't have a memory of mind control sessions they endured with these pretend therapists and so instead of rejoicing mistakenly grieve the loss of intruders.

Alison had given me genuine help, the first therapeutic help I ever received despite my having had years with cult-involved pretend therapists. Therefore the loss was acute. For three months, I barely slept. A falling sensation woke me, and I rocked my body as it expelled more grief. I would wake at 3 a.m. agitated—with a slipping feeling of black stones sliding from my heart. Parts who held these unbearable feelings began to speak to me. They took me back to what happened in infancy and before. The chronic stinging pain high up in my heart has been from inside paralysed infants. It's they who will miss Alison the most. She reached into them and they expected she would always be there. I did not understand why Alison called me to Victoria and then left. It was time for her to take care of herself. Therapists are not slaves to clients.

When I was in the womb, my mother received electric shock so that she would become so involved with her own pain that she left me. Then I felt more acute abandonment than outside-the-womb people experience.

My mother left me routinely and my forming heart burned. When she was with me, it wasn't good. No love was in the womb. Just despair and anger and so much resentment though I would not have been able to name it yet. I found a corner to huddle in and stayed there. I was angry. I was cold. I hated people. That was it for me. For nine months I experienced a condensed pre-taste of what was to come. People like myself cannot bounce back from abandonments.

And the foetus me withdrew before my mother left me again, so that I did not have to re-feel that unbearable pain. My design of leaving first led me to leave Victoria before Alison when I returned to live with my friends. Whenever someone I care about abandoned or rejected me, I had a strong reaction like that.

I needed to keep moving in order to cope. I left and went back to my original plan of driving on, not knowing where, searching, seeking. So I packed up, put my dog in the car, and left the gracious safe house offered to me by genuine friends, and drove. This was the second time in my life that I was going somewhere—though I didn't know where—on my own, without being tortured into it. The first time was when I originally drove to Victoria, years before. I felt exhilarated for a few days, because I suddenly had autonomy again. My perpetrators didn't know where I was. I didn't have to peer behind me to see if someone followed me. I didn't have to memorise licence plate numbers. I had a taste of not being afraid of assaults. I could live like a human being. I rode the thinnest air on the sweet crest of freedom through Canadian mountains. The landscape barely changed. The cliffs remained solid. No one pursued me. Life could be peaceful, splendid.

Until grim reality set in. It was only June and I hadn't anticipated the hot spell. My dog and I had heat exhaustion. I could only go out before sunrise and after sunset. I reached Minneapolis but could not find a place to rent. I could not look diligently and constantly because of the weather and could not leave my dog in the car as I looked. The talk radio shows poured out Trump-era hatred. I remembered Trump from satanic ceremonies. As an old teenager, young adult, he stood in line with other hopeful politicians waiting for a blessing from satanic royalties. His antics were known and encouraged. I don't know when the leaders decided to make him a presidential candidate. The dyke restraining the undercoating of Nazism burst in this geographic area. I am sure there are many pockets of rational thinking but I didn't know how to find them. I drove back west. My constant Canadian friends allowed me to return to their home. My feeling had begun to subside. Alison had already left and begun her new life away from much of the field. I stayed with my friends a few more months.

I worked on my own and found the Nazi section where the recently accessed parts resided. I climbed internal streams and rivers probing barricades, seeking unearthed parts and slivers. Alison had started me on a path and now I could pioneer alone.

Since this loss bled into my other losses, different parts revealed themselves. They expressed a combination of anger, disappointment, and despair. To create personalities, programmers strip away every remnant of self-esteem and identity.

These newly discovered parts repeated to the rest of me what programmers had said to them: "You are unloved. You will always be left. No one will want you."

After each statement, torture—a cigarette burn on my infant feet alternating with an electric shock—to cement the learning.

"You are nothing, you are unlovable. You are a burden. No one can love you. You are a throw-away. You are a rag."

Somehow Alison's leaving made these feelings seem truer.

Another part said: "I had a wet nurse and she held me and let me suckle, then dropped me in the middle of it. That happened often."

Programmers said: "We have to make sure she has no mother-love."

"You're the lowest. You're the lowest because you have no mother. You have no mother because you are bad."

In addition to the abandoned infants, older parts designed for satanic royalty came forward. They described how programmers put little queen parts next to space heaters to make them too hot. They placed different little queen parts next to the open fridge or in the freezer.

This current group of perpetrators used some parts at the harrowing foundation of the separation between inside and front parts. For example, they used an abducted infant part hidden in the Nazi section named Melissa. Perpetrators placed a rod under her arms that stretched her back to form her. The pain went diagonally across my spine. I discovered that she and thirteen splits comprise the foundation of front people.

Original programmer: "Keep her like this for twenty minutes. Let her rest thirty minutes. Repeat four times. Then ten minutes. Then five minutes. Don't pick her up or soothe her." That is how eight of the splits occurred.

"You must stay away from the others. You may not reach out to them." The programmer had meant the internal others.

They dropped me, held me and dropped me over and over.

"Give her the medicine and electricity to separate her."

They held a gun to my head. "We will blow your brains out and everyone else's if you ever reach out."

"You are separate from the others. You are not part of them. You are alone for evermore. I am building a brick wall between you. [He showed me a brick, a bucket of cement, and a tool.] No one has ever destroyed a wall like this." Then he blasted me with electricity.

I did dismantle the metaphoric brick wall. During the torture-programming, I succumbed to fear. Gradually, my body bounced back and my gumption returned. I don't want to minimise the pain.

I have not been tortured for over three years. My body feels much looser. My neck barely hurts. The skull's seams can be ripped apart but can re-stitch themselves. Loneliness is a shadow but also a friend. The second generation of victims coming out of mind control slavery may not be so isolated as I have been. Hopefully, there will be a second generation of escapees which will make this personal suffering worthwhile.

SURVIVOR CONFERENCES

One of the biggest problems for surviving victims coming out of mind control groups is isolation. Those who attempt escape find themselves alone, in general.

One remedy for disrupting isolation is conferences for dissociative people and for victims of satanic cults. At these conferences, participants learn about mind control, meet people like themselves, and find community. But there is a foreboding side to this agreeableness. Perpetrators also attend. Conferences make it easy for perpetrators to abduct or access victims and most likely no one would notice or help. Torture can take place within or outside the hotel in rituals or privately. Imposters have a whole group of victims in one place to torture and reprogram. And these are some of the best victims, because they want to learn what happened to them and escape.

Moreover, the administrators and leaders of many of these conferences are double agents. Their front personalities help victims, but their inside ones arrange to have perpetrators give some of the lectures and presentations. The organisers report what rooms the victims sleep in, and turn a blind eye to the torture occurring on and off the premises or participate in it. Possibly one of the few surviving victims who is not a double-agent-administrator of conferences, possibly the only one, is

Neil Brick who volunteers for Survivorship and SMART. Neil means to bring these issues to light for the right reasons. Consequently, he is constantly harassed by enemy groups. But even he cannot keep all the attendees safe during the whole conference.

I went to a 2014 conference on ritual abuse near Chief Rain-in-the-Face, while I remained a prisoner in Liz's home. I hadn't yet realised what happened to me there and did not know that Liz and Hank (not his real name) were perpetrators. They also attended a conference run by the Survivorship organisation, where Hank presented. I attended two Survivorship conferences, in 2016 and 2017, where I presented, once about infiltrators.

Conference near Chief Rain-in-the-Face

Saturday early morning during this conference, while I slept at Liz's unsafe house, these perpetrators held a gun to me, tied my hands behind my back, and carried me to a car. They placed a drug cloth over my face and I went from terror to unconsciousness. My brain floated five miles away and I crawled through dark alleys but still couldn't find it.

When I came to, I was at an outdoor ritual tied to a tree, near a fire, and naked with my heart galloping through the drugs. Before they blindfolded me, I saw Liz, her friend who exhibited at the conference and also stayed at Liz's house, the administrator of the conference, her therapist, one of the famous, glorified speakers, and Liz's husband, plus the Prim contingent whom I hadn't met yet, as well as several probably local victims. They all chanted:

> "Stinken, stinken, rotten queen,
> Sticken, stinken, rotten queen,
> Into the garbage pail,

Now spin and spin [they ran around me]
Now spin and spin

Down with your arms
Down with your wings
Down with your skin
Down with your feet
Down with your legs

Stinken, stinken, rotten queen,
Sticken, stinken, rotten queen,
Into the garbage pail,
Now spin and spin [they ran around me]
Now spin and spin

Praise Liz
Praise Hank
Praise Jeff
Praise Ann

Down with the witch
Down with the bitch
For evermore."

I perched high on a tree, found a nest, and squeezed in. I became a bird in a loving flock.

They threw buckets of unpleasant fluids on me, then hosed me down which hurt my breasts especially.

While these victims in black robes chanted, I screamed at them not to follow orders, that freedom is possible, that they were mind controlled. I must have sounded like one of those missionaries on street corners. At least I did that. To stop me, Liz in her meanness and fury kept injecting me which came close to killing me. I could have been thrown in a ditch somewhere but it didn't happen. They would have been cruel to Blossom if she remained with them after I was gone.

They removed my blindfold:

> "Look who hates you
> Look who despises you
> You are ours now
> We will despise you
> Eventually kill you
> And chop you to pieces
> Now and for evermore."

I noted people I knew and strangers.

Shortly after I moved to Prim, when I had been ordered to meet the head of the coven there, my mind flashed on her in a black robe from this ritual, but my front mind didn't develop the information. I had not yet trained myself sufficiently to listen carefully to my muffled, innermost knowledge.

Had I not been living in Chief Rain-in-the-Face and Prim, they might have never found out where I had moved to. It is possible to get away from them.

After the conference, in Liz's house, she tied my wrists together, held a knife to my jugular, and Jeff held a knife to Blossom.

Liz: "You have no friends. Everyone on earth is your enemy. No one on earth will ever help you. You may never go to another conference. Never. If you ever go to another conference, I will kill you and Jeff will kill Blossom. Stay home where you are safe. We will be checking up on you."

Even if you feel hopeless during programming, you can regain yourself and hope as you recover.

I did find people to help me and I did go to other conferences, even presented at them. You can sometimes identify satanic mind controlled perpetrators by the coldness underneath their manipulations and amoral rages. It takes more looking to find their terror.

"Your rubbery tongue will never speak again.

It is all a waste, waste.

Everything is a waste for you.

You are stupid, ignoramus.

How much money did you give Alison?

For nothing.

Look at you now, lying here on the floor, ignoramus."

Blossom started barking.

"Jeff, kill the dog." I screamed "NO." Liz said gag her. The guest in her house gagged me, tied my legs with rope, and wrapped them in plastic. A drug paralysed my legs.

Hank held a gun to me the whole time.

"I have consulted with the highest council. They gave you an expiration date. While everyone else is off at conferences doing some good in the world, you will be alone at home and that's when and where you will kill yourself. It could be any conference—there are many each year. Choose one, preferably the next one, and do yourself in. You will be helping humanity. All survivors will applaud you."

Their supervisor sauntered in and ordered my healing work undone:

Carl: "Cut the strings inside. All parts must go to their original places. Undo everything from Alison's. Sever all ties." He showed me a puppet. Liz pushed the gun in my stomach.

Carl: "Have you done it?" he asked me.

Me: "Yes." (I hadn't done it.)

Carl: "Then we won't have to kill you and the dog."

Liz: "Puppet, puppet, Wendy puppet

Ugly, ugly, Wendy ugly

Stupid, stupid Wendy stupid

Puppet Wendy for evermore."

The programmer moved fingers of his right hand back and forth in front of my face: "You were asleep the whole time. You are dreaming. You never left this bed. Everyone in this house is innocent. You were nowhere but here. Everyone loves you. You have nothing to fear. You have nothing to remember. If you ever remember, remember we will kill and destroy the simpleton Alison, the wretched witch, the ignoramus, the cunt."

That is one of the patterns programming takes: humiliate, command not to know, not to remember, and threaten to hurt someone you love. To be helped, you may need a competent therapist, but as you can see, perpetrators will increase their badgering and worse because you are in therapy with a competent therapist.

It doesn't happen just to me. Other victims of satanic cults are assaulted regularly at conferences on this topic. Some have told me of their bad experiences. In addition, online discussion groups where surviving victims can post as a way of interrupting their isolation may sometimes be helpful, but they are heavily infiltrated and leave surviving victims open and vulnerable. Infiltrators try to ascertain members' locations and handlers read the posts to get information. Some false or misguided members post suicide cues or symbols that mean "return to us" or "don't remember" or "don't believe yourself".

When I assumed the job of moderator, I immediately became aware of infiltrators' rampant triggering and accessing. Neil Brick and I and later Alison helped clean it up but no online means to communication is ever completely safe. Victims' attempts to decrease their isolation may make things worse temporarily.

2016 survivorship conference

At the first Survivorship conference I attended, Liz sat centre in my audience and conspicuously moved her third finger of her right hand up and down as I presented. My inside queens registered why she came to this conference: to trigger me to suicide through her hand signal. She was probably there to torture other victims as well. Liz asked whether mind control would fade if people weren't accessed. She must have meant the question as a taunt.

When alone in my hotel room, my mind went back to childhood programming for suicide. Max had called out a little queen part: "Alexandria, you have no reason to be alive. You have no purpose. Your cousin wants your job. Why not let her have it? If you won't follow my prescriptions, you might as well follow the angel to your destiny. When I move my third finger of my right hand up and down seven times, you will know to follow the angel." The angel refers to the vision of an angel we are supposed to follow to our death. Programmers show children this angel with specific instructions on how to commit suicide.

After the conference ended, in the early hours of the morning, someone knocked on the hotel door, and my conference roommate Christine, a pretend "friend" from Prim, opened the door. My front parts did not know at that time that this "friend" was also cult and used as a stooge. The East Coast programmers and torturers pushed in. They must have flown in from New York as they used to fly to Victoria to program me.

They waved flags—swastika, skull and crossbones—to call out the Nazi section implanted in my brain and specific parts such as my Featherhead. Dan, the lawyer in training to be a doctor and probably a doctor by now, removed a bottle of pills from his pocket and wanted to pour them down my throat.

Eli, my former cult husband, said "No. It's too dangerous."

"Christine will take the blame. It won't come back to us," Dan said.

Faith: "She should be dead. We'd all be better off if she was dead and not have to make these ridiculous trips."

Eli: "Not now, later." He injured my inner jaw and ear. "You take the back, I'll take the front."

Dan: "No, you take the back."

Eli: "OK. Whatever you want."

Eli was the leader and controlled people by seeming to give in to them. He used to call men "chief".

Dan: "Christine, inject her arm. It's OK if you leave a bubble in. Now rub your hands over her neck, cheeks, throat, both arms. I want your fingerprints on her."

Christine leaned into the corner of the room by the window, afraid. She is not co-conscious yet and had said she is proud of how courageous she was to go with me to this conference. She didn't know she has the same background and was ordered to attend this conference. Did they want to kill her for some unknown reason? Perhaps she was close to breakthrough memories. But they also murder indiscriminately.

The intruders did the Nazi-based bat programming that Liz used. Eli hit my ear with a bat and said: "You will never go to another conference. You will never talk to survivors again. You will never write another word. You are finished. You are nothing."

I passed out and stayed unconscious until morning when I remembered nothing. On the plane ride home, I had a searing earache and thought airline travel made my ear hurt.

This is another formula for mind control reinforcement: drugs, gun, interrupted sleep, a stooge to take the blame for murder, sexual and physical abuse.

Eli: "If she dies, Christine, it's on you."

Before the conference, Cheryl, the head of one of the helping organisations on the West Coast, emailed me and requested I talk with one of her clients, Maggie, who she said had a background like mine. She said Maggie was also assigned the role of one of the queens of a satanic county or division of the world. I agreed to meet with her client at the conference. I saw the imprint of "royalty" on her but our interview was interrupted. Later I stood at the top of the stairs and saw Liz and Hank with the "royalty" surviving victim on the second floor stairway. Liz held a playing card in her hand, a heart, and Hank held a spade.

"Get away from her," I screamed.

Liz dragged her into the corridor as Hank rushed up the steps and pulled me down and into a room. He slapped my face and kicked me. He moved the middle finger of his right hand, giving me the suicide command, then other hand signals.

He used the bat on my right ear:

"You never saw this. You never saw anything. You ran down the other staircase. You're sitting in the cafeteria now. You saw no one. You saw nothing."

Liz returned and they threw me into the hall of the hotel. I didn't see that other victim again. Neil told me she abruptly left.

They must have been waiting in the stairwell for me with the playing cards exposed in their hands. They knew I would try to save the other victim. Perhaps their purpose in this charade was to teach me not to attempt to help survivors. Or perhaps they wanted to punctuate my meeting this young woman so that they could refer to her in future programming. Whenever you discover a planned scene, ask your inside parts what is the purpose of this scene. That will help you understand what your enemies want from you and what you have to resist.

In programming, there are no chance encounters. When you get a sense of people's frozen motion that starts moving just when you appear, you can probably assume they are waiting for you to play out their scripted scene. A part or parts of this victim must have been in on it. Controllers manipulate victims to betray themselves.

For a time, I felt like I had lost my healing, all my hard work during that year in Victoria.

I had a conversation with queen parts inside me: Iphigenia, Phoenicia, Croatia, Alexandria, Philomena, Cassandra. They repeated some of the programmed lies they were drugged and tortured into believing:

The abusers told Philomena: "This is how it will always be. You will always be unloved."

121

The rest of me answers: "I'll never leave you because you are me and I am you. When I die, you'll die and when you die, I'll die. The others left you because they were people other than you, but I am you and you are me. You don't have to be so scared and always running."

Her: "If I budge from here, they'll burn me alive."

Me: "It's not so. They were scaring you."

Her: "They'll squeeze my head to pieces."

Me: "It's not so. They would have to do that to my head and I would know. I can protect myself now, which means I can protect you."

Alexandria: "They'll pull me limb from limb apart."

Me: "Not so. Your limbs are my limbs. We're in this body together."

Croatia: "They'll tell the world who I am."

Me: "It's not your shame. It's their shame."

Alexandria: "Everyone will smell shit on me."

Me: "You smell delicious."

Phoenicia, experiencing a falling feeling: "A friend said we were a bad person, that was another loss."

Me: "That friend is injured like us. Sometimes we're not rational too."

Iphigenia, anguished: "Why couldn't we have had the same life as other people? Why did this happen to us?"

Me: "Our blood line got trapped a long time ago. One person's bad decision that was hard to undo. It is a tragedy."

Them: "It would be better to be dead."

Me: "We'll be dead soon enough. Alexandria, is that you talking? When you die, we all die."

Them: "It's all of us talking together."

My heart is spasming. Don't come together until you've expelled the pain.

Them: "We need to join together. The queens do. Not with you yet."

That is how integration works. Parts first join among themselves, then with the front or integrated section. Perpetrators torture excessively to break the victim's will which, along with drugs, makes the victim more pliable and unable to remember. For a while, but then some remember.

I'm passing stones from my heart.

Me: "You don't need to hold onto the pain anymore. You're with me now and we'll always be together."

Many are shaking from fear and electricity.

"That's OK. Shake it out of your system."

Them: "Other people look so content and balanced. It's not fair that some have everything and others like me nothing."

Survivorship conference 2017

By 2017 I knew how criminal groups took advantage of conferences for victims coming out of mind control. At first I decided to cancel my agreement to speak at this conference. But then the outrage of what this enemy group had done to my life set in. I didn't do the work I did and take the risks I took to end up a prisoner in someone else's home, not able to take a walk on my own or go to a conference I had promised to go to. I was at least as silenced now as I had been before, maybe more so. I could not tolerate this situation.

Alison and my friends pressured me not to go to this conference. If I had thought I'd be killed, I wouldn't have gone. If they broke into my room, I hoped I was integrated enough to handle it.

At the conference, Alison did her swansong teaching and people seemed to learn from it. She was about to retire and leave Victoria.

I felt communion with the other surviving victims even though I didn't know their names and would not see them again. Being part of a group fills you with a sense of belonging. My inside beings yearn to be with others like myself.

Cheryl, the head of a West Coast survivor organisation, had prearranged a meeting with me to happen right before Alison's presentation. She said the woman with her, supposedly Maggie, was the royalty victim I had met last year. But this Maggie looked heavier, more muscular, cruder, like a torturer. All my suspicions rose, but I played along. Neil was doing administrative work nearby and watching. He often interrupted. After a long time, he said he had to go back to his room and I felt in control enough to agree to remain there alone with them. As soon as he left, they accelerated their efforts to get me outside to "get some sun". They assumed I would follow them blindly outside like I did with Liz in the airport near Chief Rain-in-the-Face. I wonder which perpetrators would have been waiting for me outside, probably in a car.

The designers must have expected resistance because they armed these messengers with a plan B. Supposedly Maggie gave me her journal notes to read. As she left, she pressed on my left shoulder three times using her fingers as specifically as a surgeon, forming a triangle, which means meet me outside.

I asked my inside child parts how they had been trained to respond to that left shoulder trigger. Getting memories from a fused mind is slow. They no longer pop up but have to climb through dense seaweed and debris and finally get to the worn raft rotting in the ocean. When I was a child, Max and an uncle had given me hand signals like the one Maggie used, an obedience code Max put in Iphigenia.

Three presses forming a triangle = go outside.
Three presses with one going to the right = go to the right.
Three presses in a line, starting at the bottom = go forward, go straight.
Three presses in a line, starting at the top = go backwards.
Three presses on a slight angle going to the left = go up the hill.

124

Three presses on a diagonal starting at the top = go down the hill.

Then verbally—go to pole 5. (All their poles were numbered.)

If I didn't move fast enough, Max or an uncle would sock my face. My lower lip bled. So the feeling of a chapped lower lip that I often experience is really this personality's body memory of a bleeding, cut lower lip.

When the child me returned to the apartment after this training in the basement, my family gave me orders. An uncle told me to go to my bedroom. My mother stood in the doorway and told me never to ask her for anything. My sister told me to pick up her clothes and give her my money. I had to obey, and fast. They were checking to make sure I was a sealed child robot.

But I didn't go outside when Maggie gave me that hand signal. I've come a long way since the Alaska trip.

Cheryl and Maggie had one shot to do specific programming. I had been writing my second memoir while at Liz's. She must have read what I wrote. The reason for that memoir, *White Witch in a Black Robe*, is to expose the satanic influence from the ruling bodies in other countries especially the UK. I described what happened in the basements of the palaces and even what happened on the main floor of the larger palace. Since this training was Nazi based, they especially wanted it silenced. Maggie's journals that she left with me described a film and programming that I endured before I left the UK, and at Purple Fields in the US after the world tours. Her controllers must have thought that my reading the descriptions of my programming would activate my original programming. Included in both the original programming and her journal entries were statements like:

"You were never at any palaces anywhere. Never."

"This movie helps you remember you were never anywhere but home."

Neil said Cheryl and Maggie left angrily after the failure to get me outside. They were not interested in the presentations that followed. They probably were punished for my not going outside with them.

After her three presses on my left shoulder, I sat stunned. I looked around the conference room and chose a table by the window, took a bottle of water that I couldn't open and started doodling spiders' webs as I listened to Alison's last presentation. I thought my doodle-drawings had to do with the attempted programming I had just experienced, but the doodles released an old memory:

I was back with Mengele at both four and twelve years old. He strung threads by pulling and lacing them horizontally and weaving a spider's web around my head and body.

"You are nothing, you are a fly, I'm going to swat you, I'm going to squash you, I'm going to squeeze you to bits, to bits."

"No one will ever love you. If anyone loves you even for a day, they will change their minds and swat you away. Off, off, get away. You're a nuisance. Be gone!"

"You are not a superior being. You are nothing. A worm to be stepped on. A fly to be squashed."

So the spider's web drawings expressed my grief about Alison's imminent, permanent departure. I thought of myself as an unlovable fly.

Apparently, my brain thinks waning relationships are more urgent than attempted torture and fresh mind control. How starved I am! I never had a parent's love. I received no empathy growing up, only invasion. Receiving empathy makes people strong. At the moment there should have been empathy, there was more cruelty.

People coming out of mind control have to decide whether the dangers are worth the benefits of conferences and online discussion groups. If you have a safe person with you who will hawk-watch you every second, you may remain safe, unless someone drugs that safe person. On the other hand, not being able to go to conferences where valuable information may be gained is another form of being kept in a cage.

MORE MEMORIES

Doing a life review from a dissociated life is different from examining one from a normally remembered life. A year or years can go by without new memories or internal discoveries, then a bleak one may appear. Parts from the brain may erupt that have not lived the life the rest of the brain lived. They are sprung into a contemporary world. They may know the native language but almost everything else is foreign. They may not have even chosen to reveal themselves at this moment. When the brain evacuates its mind controlled parts forcing them to join the healed part of the mind, they follow a set order. When you are next, you go, ready or not. The process is not random. It is structured and precise. So here they are, parts of the brain who have lived as prisoners most of their lives and are suddenly exposed.

Surviving victims experience traumatic emotions, body sensations, and narratives in different sequences. Every newly discovered thread of personalities comes with a lifetime of memories. Because I knew these groups' actions and lack of principles, the narrative of the new memories didn't shock me, but their inherent emotions and body sensations were still hard to bear. I usually get the body memories and traumatic emotions first, and then the narrative. For a while, I don't know the context of what I am feeling and whether it is current or from the past. Do I really have a cold or a headache, am I really devastated and sobbing, or is it a body memory from what is coming up?

In these deeply buried recent memories stationed below my heart, I was pregnant. Weeks before the narrative emerged, my body bloated and I ate all day—sweets, ice cream, pretzels, chips, biscuits. I was thirteen years old in the memory and this frozen part of my mind.

One of my roles in this criminal cult was to produce an heir who would be part of the ruling body and perhaps eventually one of the leaders of the satanic world. The father of this unfortunate child could be a male in a parallel position to mine (king to my queen) but my biological father (who was also my mother's biological father) wanted notoriety and fame. He resembled male dogs' scratching as they spread their eliminations into the wind so that the whole neighbourhood or world would know of their existence.

I was about to be sent to a fake monastery to breed babies for their kingdom. But first my biological father had to resurrect his presence and authority. Even though these are secret cults, events among members are often public and take place in front of spectators who are often relatives and "upstanding" community members. A long-standing European tradition was that court members watched the consummation of royal marriages. For ordinary life royalty, copulation took place in castles and palaces with the court in attendance and applauding. In my hidden royalty life, this criminal act took place in a drab, garden apartment with many of the relatives cheering.

Mind controllers placed this whole episode of my life in an imaginary internal fortress-castle, grey stone with many turrets. It had four wings and each wing housed different episodes, feelings, and personalities sequestered from the rest of my life.

This discovery started with intense anxiety, my body shaking, heart terrorised, scalp feeling pierced with needles. When

128

young, I was afraid that my body would shake uncontrollably in public. The leaders thought my fear could attract attention and wanted to shut it down fast. They showed me pictures and a constructed model of this grey fortress-castle. With drugs, electric shock, sleep and food deprivation, threats, programmers led the terrorised parts into this imaginary internal prison. They ordered these scared parts of me to remain there forever and never reveal themselves again, never to mature or grow into another kind of life, to remain paralysed and isolated with a future of stasis only. But I found them at last. This hidden wing sprung out of its isolated freeze. A terrible anxiety woke me a few times during the night. Sometimes a headache. Anger. Rage. I found myself again in the childhood Pleasant Hills apartment with my father/grandfather Max trying to impregnate me. I heard myself say, "If you come near me, I'll kill you."

I had to go down all the imaginary Masonic steps inside my brain to where these emotions resided. I met an internal royalty part, Queen Alexandria, Masonic-political, who told me how she gave birth and murdered. Throughout the pregnancy I knew that I would murder the baby to prevent it from having a life like mine or most likely worse, for the heir would have been more "elevated".

Naked Max wore a jewelled robe and crown. My male cousin helped to remove them right before the ritualised rape.

I had stolen a dagger meant for a Pleasant Hills ritual and hid it under my bedcovers. He raped me in my own bed. As I screamed "I want you dead," I aimed for his heart but missed. The dagger stabbed him in his left shoulder.

They all watched: mother, sister, Max's ordinary life wife, my legal father's Nazi side of the family, relatives whom I hardly saw, the local programmer and her husband.

In their everyday life, most would know nothing of what they participated in, willingly or not, but in that moment they knew and watched and cheered like townsfolk during the European mass murders who watched and cheered while live victims were forced into graves in the heart of their own towns. Citizens witnessed the graves move and no one interfered. In this world is a long history of particularly vicious cruelties and inherited shame.

Bystanders have power. They either help victims stay connected to society or withdraw permanently. Even a protest shout of "No" makes a difference.

Satanists do horrible things with self-righteousness and entitlement. They have rituals to justify their crimes. Female children are only wombs to them, wombs to use any way they want. Male privilege. Female nothingness.

No shame or even pity for me came from this mass of relatives. They showed mostly awe for the ceremony. I was an object, a naked child to be tossed around and used against my will. They did not permit me a will. It is still going on today, with other children.

Afterwards they transported us to Bear Mountain, for the follow-up outdoor ritual that hundreds would participate in. There they hoisted me and this father in the air.

They keep pregnant children imprisoned and hidden. My cell was my bedroom, bathroom, and hall to the rest of the apartment. The family kept that door locked. The blinds were drawn. I could stick my head out of the window only at night.

I go about my day now, in 2020, and body and emotional memories sliver out unexpectedly. For weeks I had been feeling bored. For two days, I'd been eating constantly as if I were pregnant.

I couldn't go outside once I showed. They took me to the family doctor in the beginning, then he came to the bedroom. I was incredibly bored. I paced the room around the beds, even walked into the closet. My legs were still very shaky from polio I had recently succumbed to.

In another wing of the fortress-castle, I found escape memories.

I took sheets off my sister's bed. She was at college having a life. I tied them together and to the front leg of her bed by the window. I flung them out of the side window and with my big belly descended. My arms were weak from polio and I slid down the rope and fell to the ground. I wore school clothes. I knew there were guards around so I didn't go through the gate. There was some moonlight. It was cold. I clung to the outside brick walls and tried to dissolve into the shadows. I didn't know where to go. Police were involved in the group and in this episode. No laws protected me. I left the sheets hanging there.

I walked through the waterfall. My shoes, socks, and clothes were soaked. I hid in alcoves of buildings along 108th Street. A German shepherd dog found me, licked my face and hands. Animals are better than people. When they dragged me back, they kept me drugged in a straitjacket, with someone sitting in the room with me not to prevent escape as much as suicide.

They used injections and pills. An uncle prised my mouth open and Max squirted a red liquid in through a dropper, perhaps an antibiotic or a tranquilliser. Maybe I had pneumonia. I drooled constantly and looked around dazed.

The baby was born during a winter ritual. I named him Roger after an inconsequential boyfriend of my sister's. I wanted this baby to be inconsequential and not have a life like mine.

"Hail to the heir, hail to the queen. Hail to the queen's womb, hail to the king."

They sat me on a jewelled throne. I wore a jewelled crown and held my newborn in my arms. Swords clanged over my head. I smiled and nodded in a queenly manner so that they would think I cooperated. No one knew my plan.

"Hail to the leader of the new world. Hail to the heir of the kingdoms. Hail to our messiah. Hail to the mother of the heir."

After the anointment ritual, I was in my childhood bed with the baby. My mother was going to pretend it was hers. We could move away and no one would know.

131

My father kept a stash of chloroform under the kitchen sink in case my mother approached lucidity and became wild with hysteria again. She fought her mind control. My left breast started hurting. I breastfed Roger, kissed his face all over and said goodbye. I put a rag of chloroform over Roger's face and then a pillow. I watched the clock pass fifteen minutes. Roger was dead. He would not have a life like mine or worse. I murdered out of love.

What makes a satanist a satanist? Many of them don't believe in divine beings. Is it all greed, love of power, spite for growing up unloved? Psychosis? It can't all be delusional since so many world leaders and rich business people are satanists.

Back in my bedroom, an aunt watched me: "You can't keep killing your babies, Wendy. You have to behave. You have to follow the rules. You have to behave, like your sister."

Another aunt: "What a bad girl you are. A murderer and your own child. Shame on you."

Grandmother: "Don't do anything like that again. I don't want them to kill you. I brought you some cheesecake."

Mother: "Slut, whore."

Programmer: "You will never escape, you will never run away again. You will be our prisoner your whole life. You are a slave."

Deep down here in this inner world, parts have no identity and have cold, anxious hearts that hurt. They were carefully isolated, demeaned, and made to feel guilty. "You are nothing." You can imagine the methods they used to ensure that I did not do that again.

It is difficult to understand how adults fold before perpetrators. They weren't adults with free will and reasoning power. They all came from a tortured infant and most remained as children. Any bully can trick and intimidate children.

Then they sent me to the monastery to breed more royalty babies.

How to rehabilitate: like trees in the forest joining roots to support one another, the whole inner system has to come together and breathe love into these internal infants and children.

Life is like a long integrated braid hanging down your back. Even after you've made the braid neat and tidy, small loose hairs can jut out. Even after your memories are known and accepted, others may pop out like loose hairs. Work the little strings of hairs in. This could go on for a long time.

"WHEN THE BATTLE'S LOST AND WON" (SHAKESPEARE, *MACBETH*, ACT I, SCENE 1, LINE 4)

It only takes a part or two to start a revolution within the brain. A part on the top, bottom, or middle of the hierarchal structure can resist the programming and inhibit the compulsion to be obedient and an object of someone else's beliefs and desires.

The challenge of beginning recovery is finding out you don't know yourself and giving up your previous self-concepts.

Then you need to accept that you have had a fake life and thoughts that others imposed on you. Truth jolts you out of deception.

As co-consciousness and even integration increase in a person who has had dissociated identities, the brain becomes less blind. It sees as if for the first time. The realisations are stunning. They slay. Reality after no reality. Better to see. Better to know, even if the sight and knowledge are worse than wildly brutal. Better to know because unless you have this knowledge, perpetrators may continue to access and torture you. Also people have a deep need to know who they are. Not to know is too enormous a deprivation. Not having to wrestle and fight your mind control frees you to explore yourself and discover what you really want. You may have to give up the known in your life, including (usually) family and "friends".

A huge hurdle is to find safety. Some people from the normal world want to help others. If you are fortunate enough to have found one or two, they can make your world safer. However, if helpers say they are safe, it doesn't mean they are really safe. Check with all your inside parts to ascertain whether any have reservations. An innocent friend who knows nothing about this kind of abuse but is willing to learn may be preferable to someone who professes knowledge. But people who are overly naïve about what happens in the world may not be able to assist.

If you don't find safe people to help you, you are much better off living a solitary life than living among perpetrators and evil.

For me, I do best now hanging out with trees and animals.

This abuse has been going on for generation after generation. I don't know what started the turning away from honesty: disappointments, poverty, persecution, greed, desperation, no one to bond with, early torture, some combination. It could have been anything, great or small. That is what people become when they believe from early childhood on that no escape is possible and they live without hope. But there is a possible escape now.

We are the first wave of surviving victims to come out of this kind of slavery and inhumanity. These are treacherous steps but we are walking. Our strides echo fearlessly. We are giving birth to safety.

I have lived like a tree's bare branch enduring winter. I scarcely fully trusted a friend, or bathed in the sweetness of companionship; I never chose a career or fell in love or was able to protect my children. I haven't found comfort in a nest parents wove, the camaraderie and warmth of a sibling, support and union of a spouse. My controllers cut my careers short. They don't tolerate success that they have not assigned. I have only just discovered my own brain. I have to grow into my own being. I have not known life. Hatred is like a desert fire.

Enemies controlled every action of my life. If I resisted or did something not prescribed, their punishments showered down on me—life or death punishments designed to make me obey. I can see now that all my actions that I questioned—how could I have done that?, thought that?—were mind controlled, ordered, enforced. I was a mechanical non-human, an electrified mannequin.

For those victims whose deeply buried parts hold secrets the leaders don't want out—for those victims especially, life is not spontaneous. It is preplanned and regulated. Chance does not bring friends. People are sent to you. Opportunities do not spring up. They are devised. It is living a life that someone else controls, every detail of it, a scripted life. Many are forced to accept this life that no one would want.

Every kind of generous gesture hides depravity. Someone gives you a handmade gift only to get into your home so that the door is open for other abusers to enter. Another takes you on a shopping trip so that others can abduct you near the stores. One arranges a lunch date in a nearby town so that as you walk back to your car, you can be grabbed. A romance may start so that the team working on your brain might have access to you, sleeping and awake. Your leaders allow you to keep one of the children you give birth to so that this child can be moulded into a perpetrator used to destroy, possibly murder you. I will never be able to see my children again. You have a retired policeman help you with security at a conference, and he turns out to be a fixer-programmer who infiltrated your healing organisation. A couple offers you safe housing only to take you to a programming centre for mind control nights. The grief about not protecting your children simmers relentlessly.

Learning about your life is like falling off a cliff of lies.

Growing up was not maturing from life. It was learning programs others put in your brain and unlearning them once you realised you were a mannequin. Even now I sometimes get a whiff of a demented sliver of my mind that still needs a little more acknowledgment and care. Just because they are in the mass of the integrated brain does not mean that they have received enough internal healing.

The perpetrators mean to breed people who have an evil nature or a propensity to evil—cold, selfish, unfeeling, preoccupied with self—that's the model they wanted and often got. That is why their generational model is so important to them, so that they can breed in the characteristics and soul they want. There's a hitch: they can't get rid of your feelings so you can never fully be a robot. They have no control of a soul. A family of perpetrators can produce a child who refuses every temptation to the evil and who consistently chooses the good, even though it is a costly choice.

You can't coerce all people to go against their true natures. Underneath all the mind control is a real child who doesn't want to hurt anything and just wants love. The real child will resist what they have made her or him into. I don't think there's a single satanist who wants to be a satanist. Programmers were once innocent, tortured, lied-to children, and do their work in trained child states. They happen to have a scientific and organisational skill and were therefore made into programmers. They did not request this job. They also want freedom. They want their minds back too. No matter how obedient they are, they are also resentful and rebellious, like the rest of the surviving victims of mind control. Since they are working in personalities they don't want, many programmers will leave loose threads and not seal their victims' compartments adequately.

Reluctant programmers will place loopholes in your mind control, unsealed containers. One loose end leads to another and another. Or impulsive perpetrators will blurt out something that will in the end vitiate the commands. You will be able to escape. The structure can and will collapse. No one wants slavery, not even programmers and bosses. This empire only has unwilling workers, distraught children who no longer think. Despite its dominance, it will fail. The sins of the Church, other religious groups, the military, politicians, Hollywood, families are coming to light. Perhaps satanic criminal cults are next.

Victims who are compelled to act like perpetrators and criminals, you too can become free. You too can say, no more. Listen to the voices within who want something different. Let them lead you to what you need to know within you. It's never too late to become a free person obeying your conscience.

Except for the few "master" ones, programmers are not creative, innovative types. They follow procedures. Only a few madmen like the infamous Mengele, Cameron, Max Yuni known as Wiezenslowski, and perhaps some contemporary ones designed new methods, using more technology. I have been in the grip of severe master programmers. They have all cracked up while administering mind control on me. They all had psychotic and violent breaks. You can only go against your soul for so long. Then something in you explodes. Even normal people with innocent lives snap sometimes.

Life after mental and physical slavery also entails shame. For so long, I didn't know what my body was doing or where it was. I didn't have access to my mind and others did. And I attached to enemies, bonded with families and the very people who meant to destroy me. It is difficult to live with a history like that.

Previously I didn't trust and didn't know I didn't trust. Now I know that I trust very few people. Some survivors will trust no one. So we live without one of the great developmental foundations. It is like living without arms and takes strength. For those who have one or two honest people to trust, they have a great gift. People keep you connected to life.

Another difficulty is that you know what is going on in the world and others accept only superficial explanations and theories. They think the veneer is the whole story. They don't know what's underneath political moves. For example, they think assassins are mentally disturbed random people. They think politicians work their way up and don't have secret groups controlling them. They think accidents and disasters are mechanical and not part of these groups' creation of chaos. Knowledge also separates people.

That is what a life review looks like.

Some of the parts that have been in these secret containers for a long time may be afraid to leave. We see on TV the trouble and angst some refugees have when forced to leave. Our parts had been forced into these containers, against our will, through torture, drugs, and threats. Now some are forced against their will to leave. Parts striving towards knowledge and freedom upset internal systems. Reluctant parts may be forced out and thrust into life because others inside want to heal and become whole. It is like a newborn having to go to a shopping mall. A tortured newborn. Other parts will have been waiting, yearning for the chance of escape all these years, maybe, usually, decades.

They will all need help leaving. Inside parts will help evacuate them to the integrated brain. They do not disappear. They move. Inside leaders can facilitate this transfer, or workers who had that inside job of arranging parts. It can't be rushed. Each part has a story to tell. The story needs an audience that becomes the witness, even if it's an internal audience.

The brain is capable of re-forming itself and returning to something like its original structure. During the transformation back to the natural, my brain spasmed hard. I went through this process when I was already old. Younger brains may not have such a physical response to internal changes. If you live long enough, there will be an end to the healing process. If you don't live long enough, at least you made a good start which is far better than not starting. Being in the process of gaining freedom is better than being a slave for life. This is the first time that people coming out of deep mind control have had any support and a chance. Don't let this opportunity slip you by. You too can be free. You too have a chance at clean air. Even the densest drug barriers and head vice migraines can be pierced. The insides can come to life, speak, shed their programs and commands, and return to a human state.

Without knowledge of what happened to you, it will not be possible to locate your true self. The true self always exists. You just have to scrape away the lies and barriers imposed on you. No one can permanently kill the core of you.

Once the mind and its artificial divisions clear, you step onto earth as an ancient newborn. You can figure out and grieve all that you've missed, all those deprivations. One consolation is that you know who you are now. Masks dropped. You are clearer than ever before. You have also confronted cold parts of yourself that perpetrators incited.

Being around people and noises may be difficult, sometimes impossible. Just a little each day. Then time in the forest, mountains, or beach. Tea and something nice. Perhaps ten hours in bed. Slowly. Away from bad or injured people. Some parts are preparing to die, others are being born. Such tortured child parts. I have many such tortured, chilled parts. I have many to care for.

My rage now is covered by exhaustion. My skin is thin. Any scratch opens deep wounds. It hurts my soul to be around bad people.

More of my life is sinking in. I really was a slave. I may be murdered, tortured for not being a slave. I had seen no way out of my double life. I had thought torture sessions were unavoidable. This knowledge filters up. I feel like screaming.

Most of the little bits of kindness I had were set-ups.

And most of the cruelties and betrayals were also set-ups.

Now no programming hungrily waits to destroy me. Perpetrators will have to work a little to find me.

After suffering so much abuse, life is unromanticised. Healing surviving victims probably resist suicidal programming, but may not have that much gusto for life. That attitude makes the constant danger you live in easier to bear.

Once you've worked through your programming, at least you will know whether it happened, where, when, and by whom. That awareness is a gift, though one that comes from hard work.

Just knowing what happened to you today, yesterday, for decades of your life—regular people take that for granted. For surviving victims and survivors, it can be the main purpose of life. To take your mind back—that is not a trivial goal. It entails enormous work and fortitude. To know your mind, to know what is in your brain, to understand what programmers did to you and possibly your family—to let every part speak and finally to let them heal on their own terms, in their own way. That is life during recovery.

The deprivations of these lives are extraordinary.

The main advantage of working through the memories of all your separate parts is that you will no longer be a stranger to yourself or on the run from yourself.

After recovery, you may spend time realising and thinking about how all your supposed friends duped you and were masked enemies intentionally misguiding and lying to you. Programmed, they still performed these deceptive roles. Some will remember, some won't. So many imposters, liars. Can you trust anyone from your past?, you might want to ask. Maybe, or maybe it is too dangerous. What if you let the wrong person back into your life? Haven't you trusted all the wrong people?

Survivors have to forgive themselves for not seeing, and for their conflicted unnatural brains because of what was done to them early in life. It takes time to realise you might have been boxed in and surrounded.

Even the very worst of lives will have some good moments. I have had moments of life with full saturated colour. That will be enough. I had some help. Some of us have no one who helps, only books, articles, and workshop presentations.

To my knowledge, I have not been broken into or reprogrammed for over three years. I don't know whether some form of abduction will occur or whether a false friend will worm her or his way into my lonely existence and betray me to this criminal group. I do know that romance can no longer touch me. What occupies my time, at least some of each day, is realising the lies my plant-friends told me. Somehow they didn't get me to stop writing books like these, telling my story, seeking freedom, exposing criminals including themselves. My mind is coming together, I am alone, I am free, and I am glad.

It's impossible to trust yourself when you haven't yet met your inside parts. After you've met them or most of them, you then can trust yourself and your judgment. Learning to hold onto your power and authority is a difficult transition.

I am coming back to myself. I step on flat shiny river stones, not the in-between concrete that makes my ankle turn. I have never been here before, including the second that I was conceived. My skin goes from brittle to soft. It doesn't flake like bark. It no longer stands away from my blood, is no longer armour fighting off air. My posture rearranges itself. Hairs pop out of my arms. The coarse thread that tied my mouth dissolves. I do not ask and ask. I know and know. Reticence is gone, now late in life. Who might have I been? I long for who I might have been and who others might have been.

There's a pain worse than the pain of torture. When you meet people from the non-tortured world and see how they developed, there's a crushing pain because you missed out on all of life. Even if you make the best of every situation you're in, you can never get your full life back. You lost what you never had. I never had.

I look at wounds on my body. Those brandings were meant to mark me. Now I do not see these injuries as signs of someone else's ownership. They are badges of freedom. For I am free. No one owns me. I belong to myself.

Life after escape is still fraught. These types of perpetrators don't want to let escapees go. They may try to find you and call you back, even if you have erased from your mind code triggers and cued responses. They look to silence escapees or silence them for good. So life becomes a hunt and chase. Walking through life knowing some seek to murder you is unsettling. Even if you are willing to fight to the bitter end, it is unsettling and demoralising. People want you dead because you want to be free. That is an old story, unfortunately.

How better souls suffer. How the meanest seem to have power. How the measurement of power in this world is not true and real.

But you did all you could to break free.

Only the formerly fragmented know the astonishment of wholeness. It has its own perfume—a fragrance that appears only when you climb out of mind control, one program at a time, one personality at a time, one section at a time. That is the worthwhile work, work that transforms your life and lives of future generations. A child and an unborn child murmur thanks. They need your help. They need you to reach into their futures and protect their brains. The murmuring is loud. We can all hear it.

You have set a precedent for breaking free. Others can now be the second generation, not the first. You've taken a sledgehammer to mind control. Some have been put on earth for pleasures. Others for work.

When you get out, there will be no group cheer. Victims will secretly be happy even if some are used to try to stop you. Most importantly, you will give them hope that freedom is possible and available.

Decide whether you want slavery or freedom, and how much. To remain a slave, you have to remain dissociative. In that state, only some inside parts hold the pain. The rest of you doesn't know, but some emotions trickle through. You feel like a prisoner though you could not articulate the feeling. So there is pain in remaining captured and there is pain in gaining freedom. The pain of slavery is frozen and will not cease. The pain of recovery will eventually pass. The decision is not about pain. It is about how much you want freedom and what you are willing to do for it.

How you will respond depends on what stage of life you are in when the bulk of recovery occurs. If you are young, the shame and humiliation of what they did to you and what happened can be decreased by knowing that you have a future and more life to live without the punishment of being mind controlled. It is easier to think of it in the past and leave it behind you. If feelings linger about the atrocities, you can deal with them at a later stage in your life.

But if you are old and have recovered your mind at the last minute and are in the stage of life when you are doing a life review anyway, then some issues of your life become particularly painful. There is scant future. You especially agree that it is better to know than to remain a robot. The end is filled with awareness and the awareness is shocking and grim. But there is relief in knowing and pride in having knit your mind back together. Knowledge of what happened in your life brings dignity. It brings a self!

Not trying to escape brings on a moral emptiness and decay. It's a choice we prisoners have to make. Not trying to escape is a choice too. People should know what they are getting into, even if this knowledge discourages them.

I have escaped. Even if I am caught again, I have escaped. Lately I walk alone safely.

This is my new year, away from rituals and satanists' commands to destroy me, away from all who know my past and what I have bloomed from anyway, away from crime and pseudo-community.

When many more escape and talk—and not just care about their own slice of future life—when that happens, people will listen. Victim-children will be removed from criminal families, infants will be safe. It is beginning. Help is imminent. For those of my generation—old—all we can do is escape and talk. That is the first step and our job.

They have attempted to erase all you are, but it is not possible. Nothing can keep you from yourself, hard as they try and no matter how pernicious their methods. You have the rope to your inner inerasable self.

You were born a slave and spent your childhood learning slavery, and adult years living it out, but you are not a slave. You have been treated as one but are not one. You are a free being who only has to remove and reject invisible chains, primarily on your brain.

When seams dissolve and your mind comes together, your brain and body feel everything at once. Emotions and facts are no longer isolated in hidden internal places. You get the whole picture. All of you can feel well-being and all of you can feel anxiety. Pleasure can caress every cell in you and worry can rip through your body now. Experience is magnified. It is no wonder people without fragmented minds cope so poorly by surviving victims' standards. A few nights ago, a loud noise woke me. I felt terror throughout every cell in my body. All of me felt it, not just designated parts. That was a new experience. An hour later, another loud noise woke me and I had a similar reaction. The wind had blown candle sticks off the windowsill. It was not a break-in. All of me responded in a new way. That is what life is like for the non-fragmented.

Your past trails behind you. Before you were oblivious to who you are and what you've been through. Now you walk in awareness. People who always remembered work on forgetting. Those who forgot have the goal of remembering.

The worst pain is losing oneself. The pain of knowing, though considerable, is less potent than the pain of being someone else's property. You now build your identity on what you think of yourself, not what other people have said they think of you.

In this current land of chronic entertainments, distractions, and revisionist histories, you live with knowledge of yourself and your life. You don't try to escape what you now know through your hard work, though living with what you know is difficult. You will know your own soul.

A child born into a satanic secret cult runs through a grassy field sprayed with wild flowers, her heels kicking high behind her. Soon she'll spread out her arms, think of them as wings that will fly unhindered, higher, mightier.

A gull soars, weaves among blustery clouds, shrieks its cry of freedom.

PART II

SUPPLEMENTAL SECRET INFORMATION ABOUT MIND CONTROL

"Someone who takes my place inside me feels … ."
"It's as if someone were using my life to beat me with."
Fernando Pessoa, *The Book of Disquiet*, 2017, edited by
Jeronimo Pizarro, translated by Margaret Jull Costa.
New York: A New Directions Book.

Some of the following lists and essays contain rarely disclosed details about mind control and programming, based on my own life, but I believe these techniques to be commonly used.

This information is also based on discussions with surviving victims in New York, other states, online discussion group conversations and at conferences, and personal communications with survivors in several countries and a few continents.

All surviving victims have their own experiences. Not everyone will have experienced these methods. Some of what is stated may apply to you, much may not. The information says what might have happened, not what happened to you. It is for you to decide.

If surviving victims are to achieve freedom and belong to themselves, they usually have to face what happened to them from their earliest moments of life. People who want to understand the currents in society need to know about criminal mind control. Otherwise, they will mistake a deceptive veneer for reality. Therapists may want to understand the existence of mind control, because some of their clients may have endured it but may not yet be able to tell them. Surviving victims looking for help often go to therapists.

UNDERLYING PRINCIPLES
AND PROGRAMMING METHODS
OF MIND CONTROL

S atanic cult abuse is about making its victims unaware. Perpetrators' main weapon is their victims' not knowing or remembering what has been done to them. As soon as victims regain their minds and know, perpetrators will lose their power. Other groups also engage in mind control. The following is an elementary summary of mind control.

Mind control distorts innocent people into manufactured and artificial beings. These victims live in chronic amnesia about who they are. Perpetrators around the world have imposed themselves on infants born to these groups, designated them as property, and divided up their brains by paralysing the movement of connecting neural pathways, nerve cells, circuits, transmitters, and brain waves. Even as their bodies mature, people whose brains are frozen and fragmented continue to function as manufactured robots, worse than robots because they still have emotions, empathy, and a conscience tucked away in the hidden parts of their brain or psyche. In all other ways, they are robotic.

To be free, surviving victims need to remember and understand their programming and these groups' methods of inserting it into their young minds, and then consciously reject it.

I wrote mostly about Illuminati programming in *The Enslaved Queen* and will mainly address Nazi programming here, along with Mengele's role post-World War II when he travelled around the world performing criminal experiments on children. I included descriptions of some Nazi programming in my first two memoirs.

Unlike other forms of slavery, mind control victims have to fit into life and be returned to society with undetected wounds. Mengele must have been more circumspect in his experiments post-WWII because he had to return these children to their pretend ordinary lives rather than the barracks. Still his rape of the mind was extreme and he managed to develop innovations. He introduced flashing psychedelic lights, later used in nightclubs, strobe lighting, choruses of laughter as child-victims disintegrated, and other ultra-sadistic measures. He was consistently a madman, whereas other programmers had psychotic breaks occasionally. Parents sold Mengele their children, husbands their wives, countries their citizens.

The basic formula for the hostile takeover of victims' heavily drugged minds is:

Step one: take away any will and identity

Step two: render humans amnesiac puppets that do deeds.

Surviving victims either rid their minds of inserted programs or are ruled by them.

Parents are supposed to make their children feel good about themselves as they really are, in accordance with their true selves, so that they don't become false. That may be parents' most important task. Many ordinary parents give conditional love, doling out appreciation to children only when they obey or become what parents want. Cult parents not only do that but also denigrate their children and make them feel worthless. They take away any base of authenticity. That poor self-esteem leaves them open for mind control. Everything in cult life is extreme, and parents program their children to feel evil.

These programmers consider decreasing victims' self-esteem essential. They say things like:

"Now you are nothing. Now you are no one. You are a wind-up toy—nothing more."

To girls: "You are ugly, you are revolting."

To boys: "Your penis is small, you are weak."

This denigration starts at birth and goes on and on in ordinary life as well as during programming sessions.

Division of the parts of the brain

The structure of mind controlled brains is man-made. The brains often have a series of programmers who designed them and a series of handlers who control their possessors' day-to-day lives.

Programmers force child-victims to visualise their brains as actual, physical landscapes or structures. Perpetrators make children believe that they have sculpted their brains into a grid and that their parts "live" within this grid. They divide the fantasy grid into sections that look like geometric shapes. Within each internal section in the brain is a multitude of divisions. These divisions are called parts, personalities, pieces, bits, and words like that. They each have a job, purpose, and specific imagined location within the brain and body. These locations could be called tunnels, caves, caves within caves, caves by the river, cubbyholes, vaults, pipes, graves, coffins, boxes, wells, barrels, cupboards under Masonic staircases, inside any of the Masonic steps, freezers, furnaces, castles, fortresses, and places like that. Of course, it is nonsense to believe that such places could exist inside the body or brain, but the victims have been drugged and tortured and worked on when so young that they do not yet have cognitive abilities. They are bullied. Many of these imagined locations represent places where the child was placed when the parts were split off; others represent programmers' hypnotic suggestions or both. Some parts think they even live in other countries and continents or outer space or the bottom of the sea. These parts and pieces usually do not know

153

of the existence of the other parts and pieces within. They will have to learn they all reside in the same unfortunate body.

Each division is assigned certain stimuli to bring it to the surface. Stimuli could be sounds, smells, visuals such as playing and tarot cards, pictures, designs, numbers, letters, and combinations of these.

All these divisions in the brain are often placed in infancy. The brain has to be malleable. The foundation is designed so that it can be built upon. Adults most likely can't have this kind of mind control successfully imposed unless the foundation was set in early childhood. Perpetrator groups may have methods now to start mind control on older children, especially abducted children.

All sorts of pain are used to place and seal in these fantasy internal containers: physical, mental, emotional, and spiritual. Programmers are expert at segregating. Everything gets separated and paralysed: anger, shame, suicidal ideation, staying alive.

Torture is used to create and isolate these divisions. Torture includes massive doses of electric shock. This kind of electricity has maimed and killed children. Drugs are always used in mind control. Drugs can make people forget and take away their will and can overstimulate them to anger and sexualize them. Their oppressors also use forms of deprivation—sleep, food, praise, love, gentle touching, air. Those deprivations enhance mental anguish. This torture leaves a physical residue, which can further harm the brain.

When perpetrators summon a part, the unhealed victim is usually powerless to prevent that part from responding. The called portion of the brain emerges and the rest of the brain dissolves into unawareness. The only way to interfere with this vanishing is for the many parts to become conscious of one another (what clinicians call co-consciousness). Then vibrating connectives flow from one segregated portion of the brain to other segregated portions, and resistance to the perpetrators' vicious orders occurs.

Interior landscapes and containers

Victims are forced to fantasise landscapes within them, and parts are placed within these suggested environments. If programmers want a river, they will place their victims in a river or they will show a picture or constructed representation of a river, or a mountain, lake, castle, etc. They don't even let you do your own imagining. You have to look at pictures, now probably computer images, and little models. For example, if they want victims to believe they reside permanently in a cupboard-like prison, they will place the victims in such a cupboard. If a cupboard is not available in the programming area, the perpetrators will display a model of one. Sometimes programmers use the real setting and an imitation or model of it together.

People who held or hold important roles within these criminal groups will have extremely intricate internal structures. Many of the world's political leaders and well known people are born into these criminal groups. Many world leaders are also slaves, or figureheads ruled by other slaves. People fortunate enough to have lesser roles will have less involved structures.

Hidden parts of the brain are stored in a sequential order. In the recovery process, victims make their way to some parts by locating nearby others in the internal hierarchal order. Sometimes one part in recovery is so eager to be heard that the sequence is disrupted. Surviving victims should listen to whoever wants to communicate whenever they appear. Don't push them down and make them wait. Sections the parts are stored in are also in a sequential order. Victims are often obliged to work their way through all or most of the memories in one mind control section before tackling the next.

To unravel criminal mind control, the surviving victim meets and gets to know each part, program, and all the triggers. Retrieving parts and their memories is difficult because of the torture, drugs, and threats that if the person is ever disobedient, some ominous thing will happen. When all or the majority of parts combine (what clinicians call integration), no matter how programmers may try to call out parts, they won't be able to. If victims have found and healed all the parts in one section but not in another section, the parts in the other section can still be accessed.

You may see how hard it would be to retrace these steps to find the core being, before programming. It can be done. The core is still there. No one can obliterate it. Constant torture and manipulation change people, but nothing erases a soul. It is beyond man's reach.

Storage units

Programmers create other sections intended solely to store parts that are designed to stay hidden and not be called out. Children, too young to understand duplicity and too drugged to think clearly, are forced to give over parts of their minds for this malevolent purpose. If you have parts separated and not found, then integration is limited or not possible.

Some of my sections' hiding places were called:

> Bottom of the barrel
> Remnants section
> Held in reserve section
> Section of the irretrievable.

One section was called "bottom of the ocean".

Programmer 1: "You will always live in the mud on the ocean floor."

Programmer 2: "You will never see the light of day."

156

1: "You are ours to torture."

2: "You are ours to play with."

Some of these sections existed at the bottom of the Nazi structure in my system. Many other sections exist.

The spinning that occurs at the end of a programming session often causes victims to panic. Separation specialists can usurp instances of this kind of anxiety, and store it for future use.

Even if you don't arrive at the stored sections, you will still be able to access much of your programming and abuse.

How they place parts in different sections

Separation specialists often target significant internal-leader-parts that always have a great deal of fragmentation inside them caused by traumatic episodes. Each isolated piece of brain holds a different piece of the same episode. Specialists order these fragments to line up internally, have them imagine holding hands, name or number them, and give each one triggers, often of tarot and/or playing cards.

Then they tell certain terrorised parts to leave the line and imagine themselves somewhere else inside, because it's difficult or impossible for parts to fuse if they are in different, unknown sections.

Programmers may call out numbers 3 and 14. They may order drugged and blindfolded victim number 3 to walk down stairs. When the blindfold is removed, a programmer shows the victim a model of a container, for instance, the bottom of the barrel or a beehive. Victim number 3 has to stay in it and fall into a drugged sleep. Then the blindfolded victim number 14 has to walk down more steps, and the programmer shows an object such as a quilt. This programmer commands number 14 to get under the quilt and fall into another drugged sleep now in, say, the Remnants Section. These may be below the internal Masonic steps and hidden from the rest of the structure. The Remnants Section is like that drawer in the house that holds odds and ends. In this way, programmers make it more difficult for parts 3 and 14 to find each other and fuse. Assistants label every personality in an episode of torture and mind control and keep track of where they placed each one. Victims don't remember and programmers record.

Sometimes sadistic programmers might also command: "Numbers 3 and 14, you will hold the pain. You will never be able to love and you will go through life like that—loveless and alone. You can't let anyone near you. Or they or you will die. If you love someone, you will have to kill yourself." Victims may go through life believing this command, put in drugged child parts.

Programmers are afraid of victims making contacts in the outside world. Not being able to love is the cruellest, but many surviving victims do love, though anxiously. Sometimes it works out well.

Thieves stealing from thieves

Experienced programmers can go into victims' systems, steal parts, hide them in new internal locations, and in this way upset the unity of the recorded internal mind control arrangements. Thieves wanting power over victims and leaders and programmers from opposite groups motivate these thefts. For example, a Nazi programmer may steal a part implanted by an Illuminati programmer. Then the victim no longer responds to the original triggers. The original programmer may suspect that something has changed but not be able to ascertain what the change is or where the new location may be.

Mengele had a predilection for scanning victims' information books, which were originally handwritten, picking out the most potent emotional episodes, stealing some of those parts that held the emotions and transferring them to the Nazi sections of victims' internal world. Surviving victims may think they have completed working through memory sequences, but then remember new pieces and have to go back over the work they have already done, insert the new information, and heal more of their parts, including stolen ones.

How programmers distribute emotions and commands in the internal sections is peculiar to every victim. Another section called Government/Military is hidden sometimes behind other divisions and on a different pathway. Mine contained excerpts from the most intensely painful emotions from narratives held in other sections as well as information about well known people, mostly in government offices including heads of state. This Government/Military section implanted in me specialises in computer programming and attempts to control victims remotely. Even in the '40s and '50s Mengele had worked on remote control of humans.

Internal paralysis

The abuser groups manipulate all experiences of natural development and allow their victims only to experience what they will need to become successful mind controlled slaves. Within the mind control internal containers of personalities that perpetrators create, time does not move. Programmers cement captured parts into permanent, non-changing ages. Parts of the brain remain at three, four, six, eight years old or whenever they were separated, even before birth. This is perennial, unnatural childhood. For example, prostitutes and assassins may be created at various ages and stay at those ages. Even front personalities are not allowed to budge from their stagnant ages. Consequently, more than one front personality exists, so there are front personalities who believe themselves to be at different ages. For example, a victim's biological age may be thirty, and the leaders may decide they want a personality that acts younger or has more of youth's abilities. They then direct the present personality to go inside

159

and they create or resurrect a younger version. Or they could decide they want a more mature, socially acceptable person. Then a younger front part may be put to rest inside, and an older one created or resurrected. Any parts put to rest inside may not permanently be set aside. They can be called out whenever programmers or leaders think they could use that version of this same victim.

Developmental stages are also thwarted and stopped to prevent any possibility of growth and natural development. One reason parts sometimes can't effectively think through problems that arise is because of this developmental paralysis. During my childhood, I remember my mother saying, "Other people seem to mature, but I remain a child." She observed what her mind control did to her without knowing she was mind controlled. Despite active mind control, victims can go through natural and unprescribed developmental stages.

After awareness that comes from co-consciousness and integration, it shocks when parts that thought they were, for example, seven years old look in the mirror and see an old face. Frozen inside parts do not observe their bodies grow older. After integration and without mind control interference, the body catches up with its chronological age and becomes what it was meant to be. Survivors' minds also mature and catch up with the body's real age. Survivors may be distressed at how much they age physically as these changes occur, but being who you are and were meant to be is far more important than how old you appear. And torture takes its toll. Societies that worship youth's looks are vacuous. It is better to reflect your age than live in a deep freeze.

Reporter parts

In another section are parts that report what the person they belong to is doing, even thinking. Separated by walls of electricity, they do not see or comprehend the harm their compulsive reporting to the perpetrator group does to others inside the same mind. Reporters, also called "spies" or "investigators", hear what those parts they have to watch say but don't see how their tattling affects them. When reporters understand the feelings of the other parts they betray and also how they are connected to those and all other internal parts, that they all are in one body, then growth can occur.

Reporter parts are also used to spy on outside people, especially those who may be considered a threat to secret groups. They are told to befriend a targeted person and report that person's confidences.

One of the first jobs in recovery is to make the one-way stream between reporters and other inner parts a two-way stream. Progress isn't accomplished until reporter parts comprehend the damage they do and change sides. They can become good protectors and advisers.

Perpetrators may use technology now to do most of their spying. Consequently, they may create fewer internal reporter parts.

Front parts

On top of the main interior section, and coating it, is a long and narrow section that is designated for normal, everyday life. Mind controllers know they will most likely make more than one front person part and they have created a space within for all the unused front parts to reside. The front part that is presently "out" in the world will belong to the exterior. The others will live in this designated internal space. Some survivors will only have a few front people during their lifetimes. Others will have many. Before healing, each front part may think it is the only one. Each currently used front part knows nothing of the dissociated life and teeming death within the brain, because a thick, supposedly impermeable barrier separates it and prevents communication. The front thinks she or he is a normal person but carries all or some of the tumult from inside without being able to define or understand it.

Electricity

Today's mind control is dependent on electricity and guns. Victims experience electric shock and Taser hits from infancy on. Some feel electric bullets while in the womb. Perpetrators use electricity during programming sessions to seal in commands and erase victims' memory of what happens to them during programming. In their ordinary lives, surviving victims sometimes shake involuntarily. Their heads jerk in particular. The shakes and jerks are memories and after-effects of electric shock. As you go against a program, your head may shake.

Guns

Victims have all been trained to become completely obedient when they see a gun or feel the muzzle of a gun pressed into their bodies.

Perpetrators introduce guns into infants' lives. They point their guns at crawling children and toddlers and instruct them to stop on command. They say "start" and "stop", and children have to do so immediately. If children won't stop moving, programmers may shoot their dolls or stuffed animal toys. Children think these dolls and toys are alive and grieve. Programmers keep a huge supply. Even willful children eventually become obedient.

Programmers do not cease reinforcing gun programming. They say something like:

"When you see the gun, you follow instructions. No arguments."

"Whenever a gun's pointed into you, you obey or else."

They usually threaten to kill someone you love unless you obey, or to kill you if that threat is more effective. Sometimes they threaten and hold guns to other victims. They say that if you don't do what they tell you to do, they will murder the other victim or victims. Perpetrators create impossible situations and attempt to murder victims' souls.

Loud noises sometimes devastate surviving victims. The noise makes their bodies re-experience gun shots. As people heal, these reactions subside.

Gun programming is an important program to break because this program insists on obedience in any environment. It inspires such fear that for some surviving victims, it is one of the last programs broken.

Making children believe they are evil

They contrive ways to convince child-victims that they are evil.

They tell them what they did is wrong and slap them across their faces.

They make them wear Satan costumes and whip other innocent victims. The programmer says: "See, you are just like me. You like to punish people. You like to hurt."

When they are very young, they force them to whip dolls.

"Hurt them or we will kill you."

Child: "Go ahead."

They bring in siblings. "Then we will kill *them*."

In recovery, surviving victims work hard to change from robotic machines to human beings. Those who have not had mind control cannot usually conceive of being a breathing, eating, sleeping machine and not a human. Surviving victims and even survivors tend to be overly sensitive to mistakes they make or think they make. Diligent work on improving self-esteem may help decrease overreaction.

Names

Some of the system's internal leaders have been given the same name as external perpetrators. That naming can devastate surviving victims because their healthier parts hate these perpetrators. Programmers do this double naming to make victims think they are evil and encourage them to do vicious acts. For example, they place Hitler figures and assistants in the victims' internal worlds to pretend they control the victims from the interior. They use little figurines on sticks and moving lights to pretend they invade victims, and use hallucinogenic drugs, head vices, and electric shock to induce a near unconscious state in their victims.

They say something like: "Hitler is inside you making sure everything stays in place. Your other master will never find it. My assistant here is inside you. Do not disagree with anything she tells you. You are ordered to obey." However, those victims' internal leaders are capable of changing sides and using their taught skills for healing. For instance, those that keep parts in place may supervise an orderly internal departure into co-consciousness and healing. Or reporters can reverse their tasks and make sure no one inside spills secrets, even inadvertently. And witches can help spot danger. After integration, survivors will maintain these skills but shed humiliating, false names.

Feelings leak

The front parts are porous and feelings from inner pieces reach them. This permeability is one-way. The rational thoughts and responses of the front parts in ordinary life do not usually reach the inner hidden parts, arrested in childhood.

The way in which victims react to a current, ordinary life situation depends on which parts of their minds are forward at the moment. For example, if angry parts are near the surface, they might feel more anger. If passive parts are closer to conscious awareness, they may feel immobile. All those frozen inside feelings may hook on to one situation or another. Surviving victims confuse other people because sometimes they react strongly to what is said or done and other times their responses are neutral or nonchalant.

The scalp

Programmers use the scalp as a battlefield. Needles going deep into the scalp is another way of splitting a whole brain into clusters of controlled, obedient personalities.

They direct parts of the brain to think they changed locations as they press needles into the scalp and say something like: "You go here and you go there and you go here and you go there. One little piggy went to market." Some say "You go hither, you go thither."

"You have no mind, only a body that goes where we point."

Victims with injured scalps sit in high-powered electric shock chairs while programmers intimidate:

"You are all under my command."

"You will leave here. You will go away."

"You will always be away from yourself now."

"This will keep you from ever being whole."

"This will finish you off but good."

To increase a feeling of helplessness in their victims as needles go deep into bleeding scalps, perpetrators use statements like: "No one will ever help you. There are none of those good people in the world. You are alone and without friends or helpers. You little fool."

Children don't want to go away from themselves, and their front people live with danger under their noses that they don't recognise. They go on living with the people who abused and sold them.

Perpetrators also draw symbols on the scalp and direct four of the prime parts within to go to each corner. They make statements and commands such as: "These are the four corners of the world. The foundation of our empire. We depend on you.

We have bred you for centuries. You must obey us and fulfil our destiny." They repeat the word "obey" frequently.

Additionally, they cause pain in the middle of the soft spot, and say variations on something like: "This is where I am putting the hook for your string. Now you are my perennial marionette and puppet." Children or child parts believe anything. They have not yet developed critical thinking skills.

Duo programming with "famous" people

Along with degradation, these cults find ways to glamorise mind control and enhance the grandiosity and false specialness victims are also made to feel. For example, victims are sometimes programmed along with the famous, or lookalikes of famous people.

Some may be paired with stars or lookalike stars. Those who hold "royalty" positions in the cult may be paired and programmed with ordinary life royalty. The victim and famous victim may be placed in two black chairs side by side. If the famous person and the victim are resistant, there may be more programming in an attempt to make them both pliable and evil.

Duality, opposites

Programmers insert contradictory commands in victims' brains to confuse them and create a stasis.

Victims have contrary programming that exists together: suicidal and don't-die programming, sanity and insanity, be dizzy and don't be dizzy, eat and starve, sleep and stay awake, smoke and don't-smoke and so on, all in parts placed in separate containers. Even bodily functions are controlled. Controllers pull the string they want when they want it.

When they want one state, they pull out the parts that hold it. When they want the opposite state, they pull out those parts. For example, after a trauma, they will create don't-eat programming. They drug the victim with a nausea producing drug. In the 1950s, the nausea producing drugs were a combination of syrups, injections, and pills under the tongue. Then the main giver of food such as a mother or grandmother shows the victim delicious sweets like cake, candies, ice cream. Victims will usually vomit and have no appetite and may not be able to eat for days. They will continue dry vomiting. The programmer separates and names the part that is not able to eat and seals it. Each part has back-ups.

To bring the body out of the starvation state, they use hunger-producing drugs, the same drugs they use to induce eat programming. The drugs used for eat programming may produce compulsive overeating and weight gain. Many female child victims are underweight and don't gain weight until the programmers induce eat programming or menstruation and then may become overweight. They manipulate victims' weight to decrease their self-esteem, make them ashamed, or sometimes to hide imposed teenage pregnancies. Programmers name and store the parts forced to eat.

Program designers prefer that victims commit suicide rather than remember that they are mind controlled slaves. Parents demonstrate how to kill themselves. They paste rubber slits over their children's wrists, demonstrate how to use a razor, teach them to follow the suicide angel and use many other methods. Suicidal programming is woven throughout personality systems.

For don't-die training, perpetrators might place very young children on roofs. They instruct victims to fall off, but long ropes pull victims back to safety. The chorus sings "don't-die, don't-die". Or they dunk children in a ditch filled with water and pull them up right before they would have suffocated, while choruses sing. If they have to administer artificial respiration, they will tag that experience onto the don't-die programming.

For sleep programming, perpetrators place a rag drenched in chloroform over victims' faces, give victims drugged drinks or injections. For don't-sleep programming, they shoot BB guns at victims or poke them with sharp sticks until they wake and stay awake.

They use dolls when they teach not to love.

They say something like: "You may not love your doll. Hit your doll. Punch your doll in the stomach. Pounce on your doll. Put pins in your doll. Pull the legs off your doll. Pull the arms off your doll. Now the head. Stamp on your doll. Now you don't love your doll. Now you will love no one. It is a sin to love." They repeat these commands frequently in case victims lose concentration and stop listening.

If victims won't hurt dolls or stuffed animals, perpetrators grab and hurt the toys. They may pull the toy's hair out, hair by hair and burn its whole body. They attempt to teach that resistance doesn't work, but it does eventually.

They use certain drugs to force victims to think that they feel love. They point out the person or show a photo of the person and command victims to love him or her. Victims will already have inner parts that have been programmed to love on command. That way programmers may force victims to give their hearts to destructive people.

Romance

People do not know what love is and can do unless they are loved. Cult members are unloved people. Programmers permit no romantic attachments. If victims were to have good relationships with someone, they might realise how they are being treated within their group and want something better for themselves. Programmers feel that they have to prevent any nurturing contact from occurring. They do allow a best friend early in childhood but only so that they can sacrifice that friend and teach their living victims that they must not love or the loved person will be killed.

They say, "No unassigned girlfriends and boyfriends. No outside connections."

"Get rid of this boyfriend (or girlfriend) or you will be punished. None for you unless we send them. You are ours."

Although programmers will not permit you to have a real relationship, they may assign you someone to love. That person will be someone they have control over. You may think you love this assigned person, but you would not love her or him without the programming, and that person will be detrimental to your life.

Lookalikes

Satanic perpetrators manipulate victims' feelings by creating false scenes. For example, these groups use lookalikes or people who resemble their targeted victim to make them feel bad or jealous or to evoke despair and take away identities. They may romantically couple lookalikes with victims' spouses or partners to create jealousy.

They also send romantic impersonators who look like beloved childhood friends who were sacrificed. Those chosen because they resemble someone loved in the past can evoke feelings of longing, grief, and often guilt. In surviving victims' lives, there are few if any people who genuinely loved them. Any resemblance to a loving person creates a bond and the victim may make the mistake of choosing to be with that pretend person.

They impersonate therapists treating surviving victims of mind control and in that way try to destroy necessary trust.

Rodents/insects

In programming basements and cellars, often in government buildings, programmers make hungry children think they are rodents and insects.

They make children wear mouse or rat costumes with whiskers and crawl through mazes until they reach a piece of cheese.

When they reach the cheese, other workers electric shock them and tell the starving children they aren't allowed to eat it.

Perpetrators also train the children to bring an object to someone. Tall men in black boots surround crawling children. Victims go through mazes to the cheese and bring it to the boots, while electric shocked. Guns are held to them.

As rats and mice, they have to crawl into man-made holes in the walls.

When children imitating rats emerge from the maze, they have to bite the padded ankle of one of the men.

Drugged boys and girls who no longer think of themselves as children have to crawl into cages and go to sleep huddled together. When they wake, they return to electric shock chairs and are made to forget about having been made to believe they were rats and mice.

Once home, children will not remember, but a part within may emerge and act out what happened in programmers' care. They may bite a home programmer's ankle as a way of telling. The home programmer won't know what's going on. This programmer may not even have known his victim had been away. The victim's parents may have known their children were away but received enough money that they don't tell, or had been mind controlled not to tell.

A home programmer may be astute enough to discern that the crawling and biting tell what happened. He may put the child in the black chair and increasingly tighten the head vice. But he won't know the codes so he won't be able to get into the other section that holds the information.

Because children saw what happened to one another, this is considered group programming. Little boys seemed to suffer emotionally even more than little girls. No one thought the abuse counted as fun. Being tortured together can make for intense bonding, even if victims' other internal parts have no recall in their ordinary lives.

Group programming

For decades, satanic cults have worked on more efficient programming methods that did not entail one programmer to one victim. They desired groups of victims programmed together, who believed the same things and functioned in the same way. As their populations increase, they think they need to program faster. Governments even abduct young people from other countries, for they need more assassins, mules, prostitutes, for example, to accomplish their purposes.

Injuries

If you have an accident, be alert. It may be a freak accident, but it may also be that someone gave you a signal ordering some part to make you fall or crash or injure yourself. Some part inside may have information, even to say it was only a coincidental accident. Diligently keep asking within.

A word of caution: even before you find the parts that are trained to respond to signals to injure and hurt themselves, even before you have done this deeper healing, if you are injured or sick, don't tell. Teach yourselves not to give this information. Many in your world may be handlers and perpetrators. They take advantage of any weakness. If they know, enforcers and torturers may torture you anew. Hide vulnerabilities.

Dark angel

Victims might already be aware of the electric or pastel blue angel that is supposed to lure you to suicide. Programmers project visuals of huge angels into the programming environment. The visuals seem to go through the victims and lead them on in this case to suicide. There is also a dark angel whose job is to keep all these sequestered parts in the brain separated. This angel looks like the infamous suicide angel, but it is dressed in black. Programmers may lie about the dark angel, "This is not an angel who will lead you to sunset peace, this is the angel who will remind you that you will never escape, that you will live in the holding pen, that you will rot in your holding pen. The dark angel watches over you, sees what you are doing, hears what you are saying, knows what you are thinking. This is the angel of your destiny and destruction." "Sunset peace" is another programming word for suicide. Freedom comes from integration, and programmers use the visual of the dark angel to try to prevent it.

To make you forget, programmers will then command that you never saw a dark angel, that you never were in a holding pen.

Betrayals

Even in ordinary, non-secret life, most traumas contain betrayals, and intense betrayals mark surviving victims' lives. Family, neighbourhoods, communities, and people they meet and are programmed to meet in their adult lives betray surviving victims. Family life is usually cruel, though conventional on the surface. Most families were victims for generations. Handlers are usually members of children's families. Later, spouses often become victims' handlers.

Programmers utilise dissociation to blind victims so that they cannot tell who is a perpetrator, even if that perpetrator recently or recurrently tortured them.

What sometimes inhibits awareness further is when someone within the same group or coven stops the torture. That rescuing person may come upon the torture scene by accident or have a sudden shift in conscience or another inside part may pop out. It may take longer to realise this same person's betrayals and that he or she also sold you into slavery. Sometimes there are truly good moments in life, as when an innocent bystander chances upon a torture scene, draws attention to it, and stops it.

Even after recovery, I find that I am more alert to ordinary-life betrayals than "normal" people, that is those with "normal" upbringings. The sting of betrayal seems to run deeper for me.

Grief

Mind control is also emotion-based. Cult children are made to experience intense painful emotions. Parts of them that endure those experiences are placed in internal designated areas. Then new parts are created that spring out of that deeper despair. Adolescent and adult parts are built from pre-existing frozen child parts that usually live within a pool of unimaginable grief and loss, or terror and shock. Suicidal parts may come from this kind of grief.

"It-never-happened" programming

They program victims to believe that what just happened to them didn't happen. They repeat the highlights of what just happened, saying that it didn't. This cementing of not knowing reality may occur after each torture session.

However, brains can heal

During and after recovery, brains physically heal. They may spasm as they breathe, expanding, letting barriers dissolve and waves run into previously closed off areas. Spasms eventually stop but may start again years later as new electric barriers dissolve.

Spending hours doing Sudoku helped me both facilitate growth and quiet considerable brain activity. My purpose was to restore and enliven my brain, not to work out the puzzles perfectly. My eyes going horizontally, vertically, and around in clockwise and anticlockwise circles while noticing and thinking helped revive my mind. This movement resembles EMDR and other eye movement therapies.

Internal movement can cut through electric barriers separating divisions of the mind and allow wave connectors to flow. They had been frozen in infancy but can regain movement in any stage of adulthood. Electricity can paralyse brain connections but cannot eliminate them.

I close my eyes and move my brain from side to side, then up and down, then on diagonals. In the left upper corner, I find cobwebs. I go there and let those personalities speak. They speak in overwhelming emotions.

Try moving the brain internally, stop when it tires and rest. Restart.

Body memories may lead your healing

Surviving victims continue to re-experience what happened to their bodies during programming. Drugs that were used took away victims' will and memory. Torture removed their ability to fight back. They became like pieces of wood, and the programmers then did whatever they liked to them. They attempted to erase their humanity.

Surviving victims sometimes complain of sudden onslaughts of exhaustion. These are often body memories, sometimes of being drugged. Surviving victims may feel, for example, an irritation in their upper arms where the needles went in, or in their jaws and ribs where they were kicked. Victims often delay receiving medical care because they suspect the pain is from body memories. Or they immediately seek medical care, go to expensive specialists and receive intrusive tests when they actually suffer from body memories. Body memories can last a long time but pass as the memories specific to them flush out.

Body memories are one of the most efficient ways to find out what happened to you. When you have a body memory, ask who inside experienced it, under what circumstances and what was the purpose of the torture involved. Most tortures are performed to teach victims obedience or not to remember.

Listen closely to what your body says. It holds your truth and can lead you to self-knowledge and awareness. Your body will guide your whole recovery.

EXERCISES FOR SURVIVING VICTIMS AND SURVIVORS

– Talk to your programmed parts. The rest of you may think something is common sense, but it isn't to the parts that hold specific programs. Remember they have been tortured and drugged before they had clear thought abilities. Go slowly, taking as many breaks as you need.
– Let your inner parts answer only the questions that make sense to them. Be gentle and delicate.

Have you felt the rage of slavery?
Are you aware of having been made into a slave?
At what age(s)?
Do you want to remain a slave or attempt freedom?
Are you aware of any programs put in you?
Do you suspect any other programs?
Which ones?
Have you had moments when you felt like your real self?

Start by trying to locate the part of your brain that program or those programs were placed in. Listen closely to what those parts tell you. Write it down quickly before you forget even if it is the middle of the night. Try to record the first thing the parts reveal. Once you immobilise and distil the program in question, do not tell anyone unless you have a safe therapist or support person. If you tell someone working for the other side, your perpetrators will put it back in and you will have to do the work all over again. Take good care of yourself, eating, sleeping, and exercising, as you do this difficult, courageous work. Congratulate yourself often and give yourself little treats and rewards. Stroke and find ways to comfort yourself. This is not the best time to worry about your weight.

Should you feel suicidal, remember it is a program and not you. Feeling suicidal is different from not wanting to be alive or not enjoying life.

- Have you met good people in your life? Describe them. How did they make you feel? What did you learn from them?
- Are you aware of the landscape programmers placed in you? If so, do you know where the different groups are located? Perhaps someone inside could inform you. Could you draw your inner landscape?
- Are you aware of different groups that you believe are inside you? If so, what sort of commands and instructions did perpetrators give to each group? Are you able to name the groups or some of them?
- When you are feeling strong, you may want to start making your way through the groups, one at a time, and defusing the programs put in the many parts that have been made to reside there. Think of this work as the path to your own freedom.
- Do you ever have claustrophobic feelings? Why do you think that is?
- Are you aware of front people? If so, how many do you think you have? What ages?
- Do you have or are you aware of any inside parts who have the same names as outside perpetrators? If so, how do you feel about the names being the same? Don't reject these parts just because of their names. Encourage them to speak

with you and think about what happened to them and what they are doing now. All inside parts are parts of you and can change to reflect how you really are.

- Have you come across extremely intense feelings from your inside parts? Which feelings are they? How were they created? Are they normal responses to what is happening in your life?
- Do you feel helpless? Think rationally about whether you might be helpless in situations in your own life.
- Did you ever experience sudden exhaustion or itching. Why do you think that is?
- Is your scalp tender or bumpy? Is the area around the soft spot especially tender? Why do you think that is? Feel the scalp of a non-cult, normal person if possible. Is it like yours?
- Do you ever suddenly become sleepy or hungry at unusual times? Is any part of you aware of eat or sleep programming or any kind that affects bodily functions?
- Do you have an especially severe reaction to being surrounded by a group of people? What do you think causes that reaction?
- Have you had freak accidents? Describe them and consider whether anything about them is suspicious.
- Do you have body memories at times? How do you know they are body memories? Do they start and stop or are they consistent? How long do they last? Ask what they may be telling you.

Receive this information. Let your body tell you how to be tender to it and help it recover.

WHAT TO EXPECT IN RECOVERY

What should you expect to find as you delve into your usurped and mind controlled brain?

Expect sections imposed by different criminal groups such as Illuminati, called by a multitude of different names meant to disguise its purpose and power, Nazi which includes Mafia and Masonic; MKUltra, which includes government and Masonic (there is often overlap); Luciferian (the main religion); plus other groups and offshoots like Government/Military. They all have their own constructed sections in victims' brains and will fight with one another over control of minds and rule of the world.

Expect to discover that members of these generational criminal cults fill the most honourable, sought after, and powerful positions in most Western countries and perhaps other countries. That includes government heads. All jobs and professions are assigned.

If your family is generational criminal cult, expect your ancestors to have also been involved.

Expect not to have fulfilled your true potential because of the programming, inhibiting freedom and who you are and your capabilities. The leaders view you as a slave or part of a crop and nothing more. Rebellious surviving victims watch other people with perhaps less talent and drive soar to the top of any field, whereas they are hindered, stopped, and crushed.

Expect people in your community not to be happy about your speaking out or seeking freedom. It takes many people—whole communities and neighbourhoods—to keep crime concealed.

Expect to be accessed by perpetrators until very late in your recovery process. Your enemies will fight hard to keep you.

Expect torture. That is part of reactivating your programming process. If you stay put, you may still be tortured, including rape. It's their methodology. Until recently, there has never been a year in my life when I haven't been tortured. Because recurrent torture had always been in my life, I seem to have accepted it in the past as inevitable. Freedom stops torture.

Expect multiple perpetrators in different locations. Changing your location may help but satanic perpetrators exist everywhere, and they can travel to you.

If you had an important function in your group, I'm guessing that about ninety-five per cent of the meaningful people in your world may be cult involved. If you were lucky enough not to have an important role, I'm guessing about eighty-five per cent to be cult-based people. Sometimes chance encounters make deep impressions on people and can make you decide something one way or another, or even change your life. You may discover that these "chance encounters" were prearranged to influence you.

Criminal cult members can make up whole communities. Whole congregations can be this sort of cult. They can use any religion as a mask.

Expect threats against those you love, which may include true friends, honest therapists, pets. Don't believe their threats. They are trying to keep you in chains.

Expect to discover that you were told whom to marry. You may have an ordinary life and a secret cult spouse. Your handler or programmers may tell you whom to marry both times.

182

Expect to have your children sacrificed or turned against you, especially if you do not cooperate with the leaders. Those children are mind controlled not to respect you. They would not have acted like that on their own. Even though they may seem hateful to you, underneath all that hostility remains the child you birthed and fed, still the little girl or boy who loved you once and who still does somewhere deep and old inside.

Expect to have lived a good part of your life not really wanting to be alive.

Expect suicidal and nervous breakdown programming as you enter most new dissociated memory sequences. These are programs going off and not who you are.

Some surviving victims have greater or lesser responses to trying to break free. Those who had more of what the perpetrators considered an important or "elevated" role will have to fight to the end. They often won't be able to see their children or grandchildren again if they become free and the others don't. Perpetrators track surviving victims. Escapees are often justifiably afraid to use their cell phones, or credit cards, or to have a bank account.

Expect at last to find out who you are, what you may become, and what you might have been.

Prerequisites to healing

This book is not meant to be an elementary introduction, but the following is some fundamental information about what to accomplish before starting this difficult healing.

– The ability to take pleasure in something at least once a day. (This helps ward off depression.) It can be any act like walking in the forest if you are not disabled, swimming, any athletic activity, knitting, needlepoint, wood carving, playing cards (not triggering video games), any hobby like photography, building model planes, painting, doing puzzles, sipping tea, eating small amounts of a favourite food even if the food is unhealthy, looking at snow, sitting under a tree. Being with a certain person or your pet is not good as your one source of daily pleasure, for we never know how long relationships last.

– The insistence on being alive is as strong or stronger than your desire to be dead or die.
– Your desire to be free overrides all else.
– An unwillingness to be manipulated now—at this point in your life. A willingness to fight back.
– An awareness, even vague, that you change suddenly and don't remember parts of your life or have knowledge that you are dissociative.
– Some awareness that you are numb and not living in your skin.

What you don't have to realise yet:

– That you are living in rage
– That you wear masks
– That you have a fake life
– That you were not in charge of your own free will
– That you are a surviving victim.

Cult people live with chronic deprivation. It is all they have known. Even as their lives improve, the habit of deprivation persists. Some of the tortures have been visible and others invisible. Perhaps the most devastating invisible torture is from not having received empathy. It would be difficult if not impossible to torture victims if perpetrators felt empathy. Parents are instructed to withhold empathy. Handlers threaten them if they don't. Some withhold empathy to save their children from more severe tortures. Adults who escape or quasi-escape from their cult's influence have to learn how to deal with a history of not having been given empathy. Some withdraw from humanity. Others stay in it but remain hyper-sensitive. And others learn to give themselves extra doses of empathy. They do life reviews giving tortured parts empathy. They know empathy doesn't come from others. When it does, it may be painful because it brings up their histories of deprivations. Empathy usually remains an issue for survivors to deal with. Therapists working with surviving victims of this form of abuse have the job of administering empathy without being heavy-handed and with sincerity.

EXERCISES

Try to figure out whether you tend to protect yourself or other people. Your programmers will use this tendency to pressure you into obedience.

Do you think you have to work extra hard and endure anything to get some help? Or do you think that all is coming to you without your working for it? Can you trace your attitude to your immediate family and your upbringing? Satanic cult parents receive scripts informing them how to treat you. They believe something worse will happen to you if they don't follow their scripts. As you think this through, consider whether you need to alter your self-esteem and grasp of reality. When you see yourself realistically, mind control loses its anchor in you.

What role did your family give you? Are there ways that your life has lived out that role? Will you accept that role in the future?

If you tend to protect yourself above others, you may need to work on developing empathy for others. If you tend to sacrifice yourself for others, you may need to work on counteracting your programming by increasing your self-esteem. You are just as important as anyone in this world.

In addition to environmental influences, we have a soul that tells us how to act. Commune with your soul.

TRAITS OF SURVIVING VICTIMS

Wounded

Normal people can do and become many things. Surviving victims have to undo damage.

Turmoil within

The more surface numbness surviving victims exhibit, the deeper the turmoil within. Surviving victims in recovery are amazed at the force with which their hearts churn. Interior emotions are thick and intense.

Panic

Although surviving victims and survivors may grow to function well in the world, inside their heads are a nameless panic, mistrust of humanity, listlessness, and anger. As you know your life and observe man's nature close up, those feelings may not leave completely.

Decreased need for socialising

This kind of victim doesn't miss people as much as normal people do. They had some nice-normal times with the perpetrators who tortured them or set them up for capture. They have some memories that are pleasant enough when they think back on those times together. But when they hold in their minds the whole picture, abuse supersedes nice-normal times. Whereas normal people miss many in their lives, surviving victims and survivors are glad to be rid of the mind controlled individuals who populated their lives. Consequently, their needs for socialising decrease.

Another possible reason why they feel so distant from humanity, aside from losing their children and grandchildren and spouses and careers of choice, is that normal people know their lives and surviving victims have had knowledge of the tiniest part of theirs and had amnesia most of their lives. That means they've been a robot with a palimpsest underneath whereas others are human. Above the secret life was a false normalcy. Over their imposed identities were masks.

Some surviving victims had outgoing personalities and needed people, but their lives have forced them into being reclusive.

Being overridden

Surviving victims often find that people make decisions for them since their minds have been so tampered with. But all people should make their own decisions. After integration, safe people from former relationships may think they can continue to make decisions for survivors, which hopefully angers survivors. These relationships have to be adjusted.

Distortion of intelligence

Perpetrators do all they can to distort a realistic assessment of yourself. They will fool those with average intelligence to believe they are geniuses, and those with higher IQs to believe that they are stupid or have learning disabilities. If you took an intelligence test in ordinary life, know that parts of your mind may not have participated in the test even if the test concludes that you are gifted.

Here is a conversation among programmers (one master) deciding how stupid they want their victim to appear:

Programmer 1: She should answer wrong every fifth question on the IQ test.
Programmer 2: I don't want her to look smarter than my child.
Programmer 3: If she appears too dumb, they'll send her to another school.
Programmer 1: We have to hide what we have.
Programmer 2: How about having her answer every fourth question wrong?
Programmer 1: Every third question. I'll use the flower card to seal it. Put something up her vagina.

Difficulty forming relationships

Relationships are not freestanding; people bring their pasts to them. If you had loving relationships with your family, you will look for more of those connections. But mind controlled surviving victims were not loved. There is no mother love or inadequate or distorted mother love, which means no bonding. On the surface, it may appear like love and bonding, but abuse means cruelty. Parents may abuse to avoid worse abuse for their children, but children don't understand that kind of heroism and still experience this behaviour as cruel. Consequently, they may trust indiscriminately or not trust at all.

Although no adequate bonding exists, intense yearning for love and communion does. This yearning is often unfulfilled. This lack accounts in part for bad choices and trusting the wrong people. Being unloved may be the cruellest harm. Parts may respond to any insult or disappointment with huge sensitivity like raw and immature children. They magnify anything negative and wear no skin.

Fear of homelessness

Because of this lack of love, and feeling that they are not worthy of being loved and wanted, these children fear they will be out on the street with no shelter or food, or murdered. Anxiety crushes them. All during childhood they have anxiety about not being wanted, of having no home.

They think being out on the street would be the worse death because there would be no way to survive. They undergo considerable mind control about having to fight dogs on the street. Some try running away but it often doesn't work. Perpetrators are intent on finding runaways. Because of mind control and dissociation, these fears remain stagnant and not processed.

Satanism is about the god of hate. If any members show signs of loving, they are tortured and terrorised. Nevertheless, no matter how hard they try or what methods they use, no one can stop another person from loving. Reason can stop hatred, and nothing can stamp out love.

Heroism

Their controllers place children in dangerous situations and teach them they are the only ones who can rescue others or themselves. This false sense of heroism skews their view of reality, themselves, and their world.

Internal chaos

They glorify chaos and make you think you are in favour of tumult. With guns to their victims' heads, they order surviving victims' particularly abused parts to be glad when someone dies, and when there is war and turmoil. Programmers threaten to get rid of other victims, dump them in fields or a ditch, so that the victims being trained can learn to rejoice at evil.

To be taken away from yourself is more than a feeling of loss. It's also a twisting feeling, like branches breaking.

Psychic education

Many of the victims have witch-like, psychic parts in them. Those abilities can be developed in anyone, but these criminal cults value psychic power over all else, even money. The programming for seers starts early in childhood. Internally, the adolescent witch parts mistakenly think they exist in a frozen form, usually tied up and gagged in imaginary cupboard-like spaces or other confinements. They are stored and are made to imagine they inhabit their own separate section so that, programmers think, their minds will never be whole.

The cult's theory must have been that if they torture these parts more, they will do evil. Untampered with, most people don't want to harm other people. Some made the decision early in life to be white witches, not black witches. They are taught that they are bad and in fact surviving victims sometimes find themselves wishing bad things on people. They wish something bad but underneath that is a good, white wish, which renders the curse powerless. These witch-like parts think they have power but they are powerless. It is just another trick. Nonetheless, the witch-parts grow up thinking they are evil. These parts also escape when they become co-conscious and heal.

Ordinary life's difficulties

In general, all the humiliations and atrocities that dot surviving victims' and survivors' lives were preplanned, ordered, and executed. Few are random. Those who know even a little of their lives think they have suffered so much that they should not have more woes. It doesn't work like that. There is no lid on life's difficulties. Life bites the traumatised sharply too. They still have fires, thefts, leaky roofs, mould, illness, financial worries, abandonments, etc., and liars and abusers from the normal world prey on them also.

Victims like I myself have received so little that when anyone offers them something, they might take it even if it comes with other things that are no good. Any titbit offered them becomes everything, because they come from nothing. Parts that have nothing have no identity and feel filled with shame. Only when they have realistic self-esteem, which means knowing their own worth, can they reject offers that are unsatisfactory.

PROBLEMS OF SURVIVING VICTIMS

You may feel subhuman because you don't remember what happened to you or your life.

That is not subhuman-ness. That is dissociation, which was imposed on you from birth. It's not your fault.

You may feel stupid because you can't tell whom to trust.

That is not stupidity. That is programming that mars your judgment, observations, and thinking. And it's hard to tell when people are acting and lying.

You may feel different from other people.

You are. Most people don't have the extent of systematic abuse that you endured.

You may feel distraught that you haven't had the life you wanted.

That is not your fault. Perpetrators and possibly even your parents took it away from you. But you can create a new life now, if you want to.

You may feel misunderstood by almost everyone.

Most people don't understand the human brain, how it can be separated and can't conceive of or believe what happened to you.

You may think, with this in my past, why would I want a future?

Because life goes on. There may be happiness in the future. For sure, you will meet people who are not like satanists. Nature consoles. So do animals. Try to recoup something.

When you think of your past, you may hate yourself.

How many people could survive what you did intact? I have only respect for you, your endurance, and values. Many will feel that way about you.

You may complain that you suffer from occasional or chronic nightmares.

Some traumas are so deeply dissociated that you have to sleep to let them emerge from your unconscious. Nightmares may be the only means to access these split-off memories and parts. Thank the nightmares.

You know that some well known people are mind controlled and satanists. The majority of people applauding them may increase your sense of alienation.

Leaders place those controlled slaves in prominent positions. If you tell people about this injustice, they probably won't believe you. This is part of the knowledge you have that other people don't have. It's something survivors have to live with.

You may think there is no one to help you.

It is hard to find help. Right now few therapists are competent and honest and many don't withstand the whole long course of treatment. Few honest support people also exist. Surviving victims need help but it is often unavailable. If helpers appear, try not to drive them away. In the meantime, help yourself as much as you can.

An outside person may not always be available. Be the person yourself who communicates with those parts of your brain that have been concealed and buried. You are the one person who can never abandon them, because they are you. You and your hidden selves are one.

Towards the end of the healing process, you may find that your life has been riddled with betrayals, that your family was not allowed to show love, that your romantic encounters meant the placement of new handlers, that your friends acted as spies and reporters. You realise that even the gifts you received during your life counted as triggers to make you act in certain ways. All those serendipitous coincidences were actually planned ambushes.

The benefit of understanding deceit and betrayals is that you won't fall for them again and can now protect yourself. Nonetheless, it is difficult to swallow how fooled you have been all your life and also difficult not to feel like a fool. Forget about forgiving the people who hurt you (even if they didn't consciously know), and concentrate on forgiving yourself. Express your anger.

THE SEARCH FOR TRUTH

At first it is a gleaming pyramid buried under ash and sleet. With a little support, you will make the journey over hills, mountain, skylines, into mines, shafts, graves, wells. A piece of you trudges over ocean floors searching, diving. You find it. Hallelujah! It was all only in your mind. You sit down next to a miniature golden pyramid. You are among few people and those remain silent. They must be your pre-printing press, pre-radio ancestors. You don't cry, you don't write. You think and become immobile. This is what you wanted to know. It is much worse than you imagined though you hadn't taken the time to imagine anything. You just wanted to know who you are as if that were a crime. And now you see. You were a slave for real and an electrified mannequin. You were your own enemy. Had you only died at birth or never been conceived. Truth makes you wish for death. You shove this truth up your sleeves and go on with another day as if climbing a steep hill. What is the point of knowing? You want to help yourself and the next generation in case they still want to know. If they don't want to know, there may be another century of blindness before some desire the trek towards what is. In the meantime, you have to live with being surrounded by enemies. But once you know, you can stop being your own enemy, which has the worse sting.

IMPROVEMENT

My life has been a lie.
My eyes were sealed
and only now can I look through their slits.

I thought enemies were friends
and friends may have been indifferent
—our eyes brushed, looked down—

my life has worn masks.
My feet slipped on quaked earth,
I fell into fissures

but my stance holds now.
I have nothing and am not deceived.
I go where I choose to be.

I slid into crevasses,
pulled out of ancient gashes
and wove myself whole.

ACKNOWLEDGEMENTS

I thank Alison Miller, E. Sue Blume, Philippa Catling, and Tim Wynne-Williams for their suggestions, support and help.

AFTERWORD

by Alison Miller

I had cut down my client load in preparation for retirement, and had stopped taking on long-term clients, which, given my particular expertise gained over more than twenty years, meant ritually abused clients, because I didn't want to abandon anyone part-way through their therapy. Then Wendy arrived, sent by my colleague E. Sue Blume, who had helped edit my first book about ritual abuse, *Healing the Unimaginable*. Brilliant, determined, courageous, her work with her first and only safe therapist (me) after years of therapeutic abuse, amazed me. She had left her previous life in order to heal her broken brain, and she went on to document that healing in her first two memoirs, *The Enslaved Queen* and *White Witch in a Black Robe*.

What I didn't know was that she was still being abused, throughout the time she spent working with me, and much more so after her enforced return to the United States (because of Canadian rules limiting a foreigner's stay in my country). What I didn't know was that her personality system had been designed very carefully from birth by two different large organised perpetrator groups, so that it was possible to heal the parts from one group without knowing those from the other group. What I didn't know was that because she was a "queen", with high status in a large perpetrator group, she would be viciously pursued and repeatedly tortured with attempts at reprogramming, for years. I failed to pick up on small clues, such as her telling me that she did all the housework when staying with a supposed helper family, even though I knew that she had previously used a cleaning lady.

For a therapist to get anywhere with a survivor client, she or he needs to love that client. It is a special kind of love, akin to but not the same as parental love. We know our adult clients are not children, even if they have child parts inside, and we must accord them deep respect for embarking on a healing journey. We hope and strive for our clients to recover and claim their own lives, knowing that when they do, and sometimes before that, we will have to let them go. The relationship is one-sided and temporary. We can't promise them our permanent presence in their lives, even though they may never before have had a caring person willing to listen to and try to understand their stories. At the same time, because we love them, when they are hurt, we hurt.

And when our loved clients are viciously hurt by others, it is heartbreaking for us. Although I've been able to cope with hearing about horrendous historical abuse, I have always found the current abuse to be the most difficult for me personally. With historical abuse, I can give the good news that it's over, the whole world is not made up of abusive psychopaths, there are good people, and a better life is possible. With current abuse, I feel wounded—and responsible—every time I discover that a client has been hurt.

With my first group of such clients (described in Chapter 1 of *Healing the Unimaginable*), I found myself becoming angry and determined to defeat their abusers, who had no right to treat people I cared about as their personal slaves. Those clients were able to tell me what had just happened immediately after it happened. But Wendy's dissociation was such that she only recalled her recent abuse bit by bit, and I had to wait for her to remember and tell me each piece of it. It was agonising waiting, while she was in another country, knowing such abuse was probably still going on, and wondering what she could do to stop or prevent it when she was still only just getting to know the young parts of her who were called out for the abuse. I experienced constant vicarious traumatisation as well as anxiety about what would happen to Wendy next. Somehow the commonly recommended strategies for reducing vicarious traumatisation seemed shallow mockeries, ways of denying a potent and malign reality. Closing our eyes does not make this abuse disappear, just as recycling does not stop climate change.

Wendy's memories have shown me how highly placed some abuser group members are in society, and how much power and influence they wield, as well as how they have infiltrated pretty well every organisation which is supposed to be a force for good. As a result, I have become increasingly cynical about those who are leaders in Western society. The Grey Faction of the Satanic Temple accuses me of being a "conspiracy therapist". I guess a big organised abuser group qualifies as a conspiracy. Not all conspiracies are fiction. For many years the Mafia was thought not to exist. A conspiracy of licensed mental health professionals who think ritual abuse to be real is a fiction made up by dubious groups working hard to convince all of society that ritual abuse is a myth.

You may wonder how I know Wendy's memories are true. I don't. But I have some reassurance from the way I saw these memories come to her. When she was in therapy with me, a memory would emerge and she would just speak it out while I quickly wrote down verbatim what she said. This included conversations with or between abusers. There was no way someone could have planned out such detail, then recited it to me. After she left therapy with me, she just wrote down her memories herself rather than telling them to me. For her to make up any one of those stories would have taken considerable planning, planning which was not in any way evident as the memories emerged.

We therapists, and the other helpers who assist survivors of mind control and ritual abuse or other severe traumas, don't undertake this challenging work just for personal satisfaction, or to become heroes and bolster our egos by doing something good. We do it because we could just as easily have been the abuse victims rather than the therapists, and we would have wanted someone to provide caring help for us if we were the victims. It costs us. But knowing dire realities enables some action to change those realities. I admire Wendy's courage and determination, as she has continued to pursue healing and speak out, against all odds. I hope every reader will learn from her, and I hope therapists learn from Wendy's book to pick up important clues their clients utter when they are not yet able to tell in a more direct way.

INDEX

215